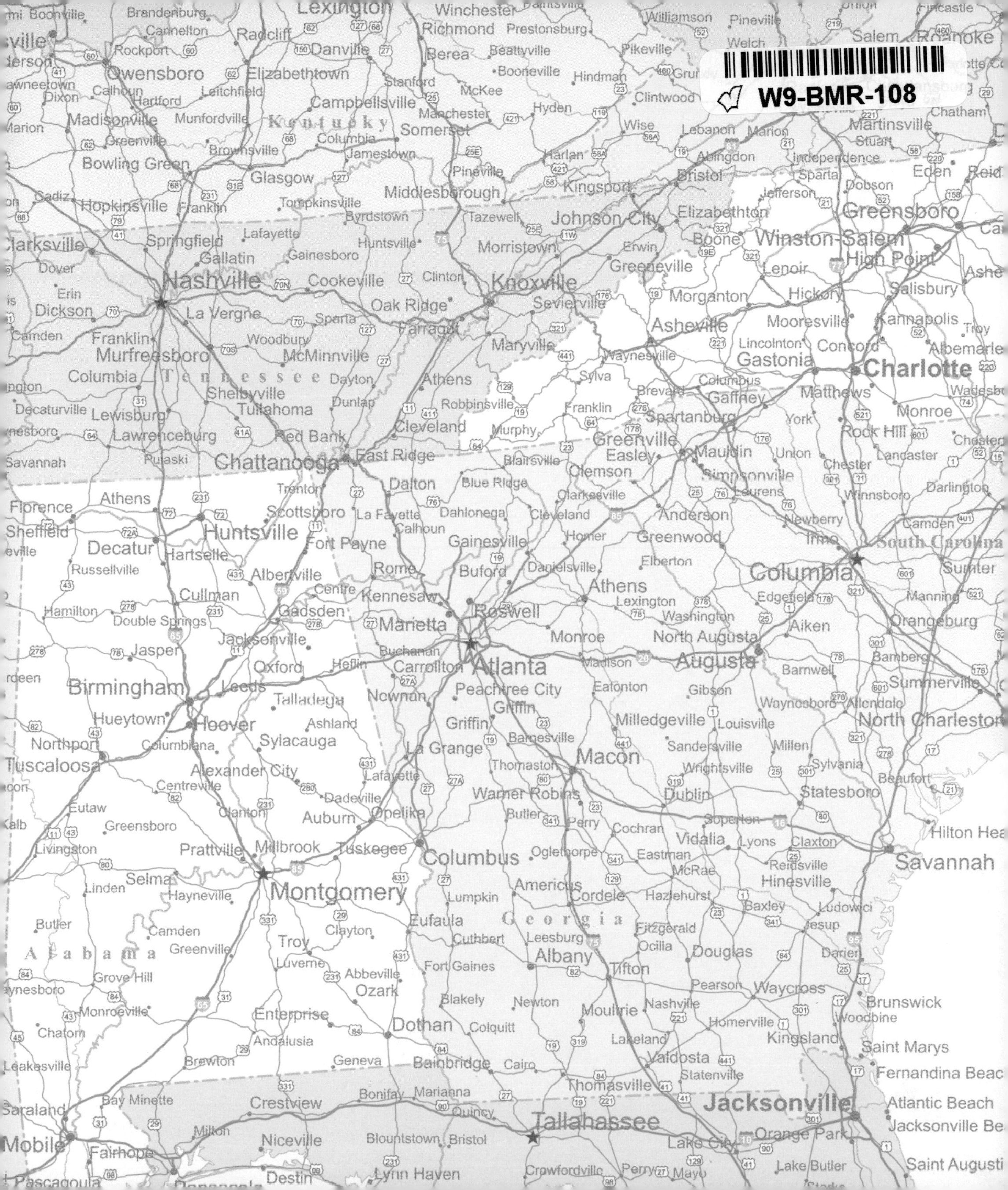

Boonville
Brandenburg
Cannelton
Rockport
Owensboro
Radcliff
Elizabethtown
Lexington
Winchester
Richmond
Danville
Berea
Prestonsburg
Beattyville
Booneville
Williamson
Pikeville
Pineville
Welch
Salem
Roanoke
Fincastle
Calhoun
Hartford
Leitchfield
Dixon
Madisonville
Munfordville
Campbellsville
Stanford
McKee
Manchester
Hindman
Hyden
Clintwood
Kentucky
Somerset
Columbia
Greenville
Brownsville
Jamestown
Wise
Lebanon
Marion
Martinsville
Stuart
Chatham
Bowling Green
Glasgow
Harlan
Abingdon
Independence
Eden
Reidsville
Pineville
Bristol
Sparta
Dobson
Middlesborough
Kingsport
Jefferson
Cadiz
Hopkinsville
Franklin
Tompkinsville
Byrdstown
Tazewell
Johnson City
Elizabethton
Greensboro
Clarksville
Springfield
Lafayette
Huntsville
Morristown
Erwin
Boone
Winston-Salem
High Point
Dover
Gallatin
Gainesboro
Greeneville
Lenoir
Nashville
Cookeville
Clinton
Knoxville
Erin
Dickson
La Vergne
Oak Ridge
Sevierville
Morganton
Hickory
Salisbury
Camden
Franklin
Sparta
Farragut
Asheville
Mooresville
Kannapolis
Troy
Murfreesboro
Woodbury
Maryville
McMinnville
Waynesville
Lincolnton
Concord
Albemarle
Gastonia
Charlotte
Columbia
Tennessee
Dayton
Athens
Sylva
Columbus
Shelbyville
Tullahoma
Dunlap
Robbinsville
Brevard
Gaffney
Matthews
Wadesboro
Decaturville
Lewisburg
Franklin
Spartanburg
Monroe
Cleveland
Murphy
York
Rock Hill
Lawrenceburg
Red Bank
Greenville
Mauldin
Union
Chester
Lancaster
Savannah
Pulaski
Chattanooga
East Ridge
Blairsville
Easley
Clemson
Simpsonville
Trenton
Dalton
Blue Ridge
Laurens
Winnsboro
Darlington
Florence
Athens
Clarkesville
Sheffield
Scottsboro
La Fayette
Calhoun
Dahlonega
Cleveland
Anderson
Newberry
Camden
Huntsville
Decatur
Hartselle
Fort Payne
Gainesville
Homer
Greenwood
Irmo
South Carolina
Russellville
Albertville
Rome
Buford
Danielsville
Elberton
Columbia
Sumter
Cullman
Centre
Kennesaw
Athens
Edgefield
Manning
Hamilton
Double Springs
Gadsden
Marietta
Roswell
Lexington
Washington
Orangeburg
Jasper
Jacksonville
Monroe
North Augusta
Aiken
Buchanan
Oxford
Heflin
Carrollton
Atlanta
Madison
Augusta
Barnwell
Bamberg
Birmingham
Leeds
Talladega
Newnan
Peachtree City
Eatonton
Gibson
Summerville
Hueytown
Hoover
Ashland
Griffin
Milledgeville
Louisville
Waynesboro
Allendale
North Charleston
Northport
Columbiana
Sylacauga
Barnesville
Sandersville
Millen
Tuscaloosa
La Grange
Thomaston
Macon
Wrightsville
Sylvania
Beaufort
Alexander City
Lafayette
Centreville
Dadeville
Warner Robins
Dublin
Statesboro
Eutaw
Clanton
Auburn
Opelika
Butler
Perry
Soperton
Greensboro
Cochran
Vidalia
Lyons
Claxton
Hilton Head
Livingston
Prattville
Millbrook
Tuskegee
Columbus
Oglethorpe
Eastman
Reidsville
Savannah
McRae
Hinesville
Selma
Linden
Hayneville
Montgomery
Americus
Cordele
Hazlehurst
Lumpkin
Baxley
Ludowici
Butler
Camden
Clayton
Eufaula
Georgia
Jesup
Fitzgerald
Troy
Cuthbert
Leesburg
Ocilla
Alabama
Greenville
Albany
Douglas
Darien
Luverne
Abbeville
Fort Gaines
Tifton
Grove Hill
Ozark
Pearson
Waycross
Monroeville
Blakely
Newton
Brunswick
Enterprise
Moultrie
Nashville
Woodbine
Chatom
Dothan
Colquitt
Homerville
Andalusia
Lakeland
Kingsland
Saint Marys
Leakesville
Brewton
Geneva
Bainbridge
Cairo
Valdosta
Statenville
Fernandina Beach
Thomasville
Bay Minette
Bonifay
Marianna
Crestview
Jacksonville
Atlantic Beach
Saraland
Quincy
Tallahassee
Jacksonville Beach
Milton
Orange Park
Mobile
Fairhope
Niceville
Blountstown
Bristol
Lake City
Saint Augustine
Lynn Haven
Crawfordville
Perry
Mayo
Lake Butler
Pascagoula
Destin

Emporia
Marion
Garnett
Butler
Tuscumbia
Vienna
Hillsboro
Waterloo
Pinckneyville
McLeansb
Newton
Burlington
Warsaw
Osceola
Mound City
Camdenton
Rolla
Steelville
Potosi
Chester
Benton
El Dorado
Eureka
Iola
Nevada
Hermitage
Carbondale
Fort Scott
Stockton
Waynesville
Farmington
Fredericktown
Fredonia
Buffalo
Lebanon
Salem
Ironton
Centerville
Derby
Howard
Pittsburg
Lamar
Greenfield
Jackson
Parsons
Springfield
Marshfield
Houston
Winfield
Independence
Eminence
Greenville
Coffeyville
Joplin
Carthage
Hartville
Van Buren
Sikeston
Newkirk
Miami
Nixa
Ozark
Ava
Neosho
Galena
West Plains
Alton
Poplar Bluff
New Madrid
Clinton
Pawhuska
Bartlesville
Nowata
Vinita
Cassville
Forsyth
Gainesville
Doniphan
Pineville
Corning
Piggott
Kennett
Pawnee
Perry
Claremore
Bentonville
Rogers
Berryville
Harrison
Mountain Home
Ash Flat
Pocahontas
Caruthersville
Owasso
Siloam Springs
Springdale
Paragould
Stillwater
Tulsa
Broken Arrow
Melbourne
Wagoner
Jasper
Fayetteville
Jonesboro
Blytheville
Dyersb
Guthrie
Sapulpa
Bixby
Tahlequah
Marshall
Batesville
Ripley
Chandler
Okmulgee
Muskogee
Arkansas
Clinton
Newport
Harrisburg
Osceola
Brownsville
Midwest City
Okemah
Sallisaw
Van Buren
Clarksville
Heber Springs
Millington
Moore
Eufaula
Stigler
Fort Smith
Russellville
Searcy
Augusta
West Memphis
Memphis
Shawnee
Norman
Holdenville
Booneville
Danville
Conway
Forrest City
Collierville
Poteau
Purcell
McAlester
Waldron
Perryville
Cabot
Des Arc
Horn Lake
North Little Rock
Jacksonville
Marianna
Ada
Valley
Tunica
Senatobia
Mena
Mount Ida
Benton
Little Rock
Sulphur
Coalgate
Sardis
Oxford
Hot Springs
Stuttgart
Atoka
Malvern
Pine Bluff
Batesville
Clarksdale
Tishomingo
Antlers
Arkadelphia
Water Valle
Madill
Mississippi R.
Sumner
Coffeeville
Marietta
Hugo
De Queen
Nashville
Rison
Star City
Grenada
Durant
Idabel
Rosedale
Cleveland
Denison
Prescott
Fordyce
Walthall
Paris
Ashdown
Camden
Warren
Monticello
Arkansas City
Greenwood
Sherman
Clarksville
Texarkana
Hampton
Greenville
Vaiden
Cooper
Lake Village
Indianola
Lewisville
Magnolia
El Dorado
Hamburg
Belzoni
Lexington
Greenville
Mount Vernon
Plano
Mount Pleasant
Kosciusk
Irving
Rockwall
Pittsburg
Linden
Oak Grove
Yazoo City
Mississi
Garland
Emory
Jefferson
Homer
Bastrop
Lake Providence
Carthage
Quitman
Gilmer
Benton
Canton
Dallas
Minden
Shreveport
Ruston
Monroe
Madison
Canton
Waxahachie
Longview
Bossier City
Vicksburg
Clinton
Brandon
Kilgore
Tyler
Ennis
Jonesboro
Winnsboro
Raymond
Jackson
Athens
Carthage
Columbia
Port Gibson
Mendenhall
Henderson
Corsicana
Jacksonville
Mansfield
Coushatta
Winnfield
Saint Joseph
Hazlehurst
Rusk
Center
Natchitoches
Harrisonburg
Fayette
Fairfield
Jena
Brookhaven
Palestine
Natchez
Groesbeck
Nacogdoches
Many
Colfax
Meadville
San Augustine
Hewitt
Crockett
Pineville
McComb
Columbia
Marlin
Centerville
Lufkin
Hemphill
Liberty
Tylertown
Leesville
Marksville
Temple
Franklin
Groveton
Louisiana
Woodville
Madisonville
Clinton
Bogalusa
Jasper
De Ridder
Amite
Cameron
Bryan
Huntsville
Woodville
Newton
Ville Platte
Zachary
Hammond
Livingston
Eunice
Baton Rouge

Off the Eaten Path

Favorite Southern Dives and 150 Recipes That Made Them Famous

by Morgan Murphy

ISBN-13: 978-0-8487-3445-9
ISBN-10: 0-8487-3445-9
Library of Congress Control Number: 2010933259

Printed in the United States of America
First Printing 2011

Oxmoor House
VP, Publishing Director: Jim Childs
Editorial Director: Susan Payne Dobbs
Brand Manager: Daniel Fagan
Senior Editor: Rebecca Brennan
Managing Editor: Laurie S. Herr

To order additional publications, call 1-800-765-6400 or 1-800-491-0551.
For more books to enrich your life, visit **oxmoorhouse.com**
To search, savor, and share thousands of recipes, visit **myrecipes.com**

Back Cover: Carol Fay's Famous Meatloaf (page 211)

Southern Living *Off the Eaten Path*
Editor: Katherine Cobbs
Project Editor: Georgia Dodge
Senior Designer: Melissa Clark
Assistant Designer: Allison L. Sperando
Director, Test Kitchens: Elizabeth Tyler Austin
Assistant Directors, Test Kitchens: Julie Christopher, Julie Gunter
Test Kitchens Professionals: Wendy Ball, Allison E. Cox, Victoria E. Cox, Margaret Monroe Dickey, Alyson Moreland Haynes, Callie Nash, Kathleen Royal Phillips, Catherine Crowell Steele, Ashley Strickland, Leah Van Deren
Photography Director: Jim Bathie
Senior Photo Stylist: Kay E. Clarke
Associate Photo Stylist: Katherine Eckert Coyne
Assistant Photo Stylist: Mary Louise Menendez
Senior Production Manager: Greg A. Amason
Production Manager: Theresa Beste-Farley

Contributors
Copy Editor: Julie Gillis
Proofreaders: Donna Baldone, Stacey B. Loyless
Indexer: Mary Ann Laurens
Interns: Phoebe Arnold, Christine T. Boatwright, Blair Gillespie, Hope Hadfield, Alison Loughman, Mamie F. McIntosh, Rita A. Omokha, Caitlin Watzke
Test Kitchens Professional: Elizabeth Nelson
Photographers: Rachel Quinlivan, Mary Britton Senseney
Photo Stylists: Missie Neville Crawford, Mindi Shapiro Levine

Southern Living
Editor: M. Lindsay Bierman
Executive Editor: Rachel Hardage
Food Director: Shannon Sliter Satterwhite
Test Kitchen Director: Rebecca Kracke Gordon
Senior Writer: Donna Florio
Senior Food Editors: Shirley Harrington, Mary Allen Perry
Senior Recipe Editor: Ashley Leath
Assistant Recipe Editor: Ashley Arthur
Test Kitchen Specialists/Food Styling: Marian Cooper Cairns, Vanessa McNeil Rocchio
Test Kitchen Professionals: Norman King, Pam Lolley, Angela Sellers
Travel Editors: James T. Black, Kim Cross
Features Editor: Jennifer V. Cole
Associate Travel Editor: Alex Crevar
Senior Photographers: Ralph Anderson, Gary Clark, Jennifer Davick, Art Meripol
Photographer: Robbie Caponetto
Photo Research Coordinator: Ginny P. Allen
Senior Photo Stylist: Buffy Hargett
Editorial Assistant: Pat York

Photo Credits: Ralph Anderson, Mary Margaret Chambliss, Josh Gibson, Cary Jobe, Meg McKinney, John O'Hagan, Allen Rokach, Scott Suchman, Charles Walton

Southern Living

Off the Eaten Path

Favorite Southern Dives and 150 Recipes That Made Them Famous

by Morgan Murphy

OXMOOR HOUSE

Contents...

Foreword

I was thrilled to have been asked to write the foreword to this book. Ask any transplanted Southerner what he or she misses most about home, and nine times out of ten the answer is "the food". Growing up in Birmingham, Alabama, my fondest memories are those of driving with my parents on long, warm summer evenings out to our favorite cafés and little out-of-the-way, knock-about barbecue joints to get a slice of that special lemon ice box pie, a bowl of turnip greens cooked just the way we

liked it, or a wedge of cracking cornbread—and yes, in my case, a big plate of fried green tomatoes. We knew the owners' names, and they knew ours. And they always made us feel welcome. It was like visiting family, and you always left feeling full and happy. Now, so many years later, I wish I could go back in time to those little out-of-the-way places. Of course, that is impossible. But for those of us raised before the invasion of the big impersonal fast-food chains, *Off the Eaten Path* is an answer to our prayers.

Morgan Murphy has given us a big beautiful book that combines two of my very favorite things in life—good food and travel. And if you are anything like me when you take a road trip, you long to find that special place that only the locals know about—one that offers real home-

made dishes from scratch using recipes tested by years of happy customers who return over and over again. Morgan has not only uncovered the places for us but has given us the recipes as well.

So whether you're age 6 or 60, climb in the back seat of Morgan's vintage Cadillac, sit back and relax, and let's travel with him on a most delightful and delicious road trip. I can almost smell the hickory smoke of barbecue cooking in Alabama, hear the fried shrimp sizzling in Louisiana, taste the zesty spice of a taco in Texas, and savor the sweetness of that fresh peach pie in Georgia. We're off to see the sights, to visit truly unique places, and to meet some mighty wonderful people. All is right with the world. Good homemade regional food is still alive and well—and waiting for us to enjoy it! Hooray for Morgan Murphy!

—Fannie Flag

Welcome...

Some recipes in this book are secrets revealed for the first time. Others are well-trod favorites. Give them a try, or if you're like me, read the recipe and then go have somebody else make it for you. (My grandmother used to say she'd love cooking if "it weren't so damned daily." That's a reason for eating out if there ever was one.)

We start 'em young here in the South.

If you truly want to learn a place, eat the food of its people. Museums, cultural tours, and monuments may tell a good story, but one bite of a region's cuisine relays generations of heritage, tradition, and family pride.

When a traveler bites into a beignet in New Orleans or eats red rice in Savannah, he or she is tasting the South's history on a plate. A fork and this book serve as a direct link back hundreds of years.

In the following pages you'll find both my favorite recipes and my favorite restaurants. Most of the time, my favorite restaurants serve my favorite dishes. But not all of the time. A great restaurant stands on three legs: the food (of course), the service, and the ambiance. Each night in a truly superb restaurant, whether it's a hotdog stand or a 5-star white tablecloth spot, there is a bit of theater.

And speaking of hotdogs, I'm no food snob. I'll eat just about anything, so long as it's been prepared with love and care. That's where these recipes shine. Each restaurant where they're served has a story, and usually the owner is right out front, greeting guests

Go beyond the ho-hum chain restaurants and explore a little.

> *"If you truly want to learn a place, eat the food of its people."*

by name (and because we're here in the South, they usually get a hug, too). They're more than just entrepreneurs running small businesses—oftentimes their tables are at the very center of the community.

So the next time you're on a road trip, take a moment to pull off the eaten path. Go beyond the ho-hum chain restaurants and explore a little. You'll be so glad you did. And if you find a great hidden spot, drop me an email.

Acknowledgements: I'm grateful to my colleagues at Southern Progress, Daniel Fagan, Eleanor Griffin, and Lindsay Bierman, as well as to John Alex Floyd, Jr., for hiring me at *Southern Living* magazine 10 years ago. My taste buds were honed by my mama, grandmama, and adopted test kitchen mama, Judy Feagin. Thanks to the thoughtful red pen of Katherine Cobbs and her assistants Georgia Dodge and Christine Taylor Boatwright. Lastly, two talented Oxonians, Phoebe Arnold and Hope Hadfield, endured traveling 10,000 miles in the back of a ancient Cadillac as we traveled the South looking for its very best food. Thank you for braving a Southern summer, many a fried dish, and more than one (okay, okay, multiple) wrong turns in pursuit of culinary greatness.

—Morgan Murphy
Afghanistan, March 2011

Crabcakes, slaw and saltines...does it get any better?

I dare you not to eat the whole thing.

State Flower
the Magnolia

Greetings from ALABAMA

State Capital in Montgomery

State Flower the Goldenrod

Alabama is near the top in plant diversity among all states. It is home to species found nowhere else on the planet.

TUSKEGEE Airmen

Alabama

Best Drive

Talledega to Eufaula

This drive takes you from one Southern extreme to another. Start in Talladega (pronounced by locals "Talla-digga"), home of arguably the most famous NASCAR track in the country. Then head South through the gorgeous Talladega National Forest. Make sure to stop in Auburn for some lemonade at Toomer's Corner, an old-fashioned soda fountain. Lastly, end your trip in Eufaula, one of the prettiest towns in the state—a place of magnolias, stately mansions, and Spanish moss hanging from the live oaks. **Length:** Approximately 150 miles, depending on your route.

Doc's Seafood Shack & Oyster Bar

Orange Beach, Alabama

GPS COORDINATES:
Lat./Long. 30.292433,-87.580963

26029 Canal Road 36561

(251) 981-6999

Don't Miss:

Famous Fried Shrimp

Doc's fried shrimp recipe (page 14) may seem too simple to be believed. But trust me, follow the directions to a "T." And here's a tip: Place each shrimp in the grease headfirst. That way, it won't curl up into a tight ball.

"It doesn't matter what you order, our waitresses give you what you need," Doc's owner Richard Schwartz says with a grin. Doc's is that kind of place. It's not fancy. It's not decorated. The waitresses wear tie-dyed tees with shorts. There may not be two matching chairs in the place. But don't let Doc's laid-back attitude fool you—their gumbo and fried shrimp will knock your flip-flops off.

Doc's SEAFOOD SHACK & OYSTER BAR

LAID BACK
LOCAL STUFF
WORLDS BEST
GUMBO

Doc's Seafood Gumbo

3   Tbsp. canola oil
1   lb. skinned and boned chicken thighs,
     cut into bite-size pieces
2   cups chopped onion
1   cup chopped green bell pepper
1   cup chopped celery
1   (0.87-oz.) packet brown gravy mix
3   Tbsp. dried parsley flakes
3   Tbsp. browning-and-seasoning sauce
2   Tbsp. Worcestershire sauce
2   Tbsp. Old Bay seasoning
1   Tbsp. plus 1 tsp. garlic salt
1   Tbsp. plus 1 tsp. seasoned salt
1   tsp. ground black pepper
1½   tsp. liquid crab boil
2   bay leaves
1   (28-oz.) can crushed tomatoes
1   (16-oz.) package frozen sliced okra
1¾   lb. unpeeled, medium-size raw shrimp
     (31/40 count)
1   lb. white fish fillets, cut into bite-size pieces
1   lb. fresh crabmeat
¼   cup filé powder
Hot cooked rice

* Diner Secret: A gravy packet and a dash of browning-and-seasoning sauce offer a shortcut substitute for making a roux.

1. Heat oil in a large stockpot or Dutch oven over medium-high heat. Add chicken; sauté 5 minutes or until browned. Remove chicken, reserving drippings in stockpot. Add onion, bell pepper, and celery; sauté 4 minutes or until tender. Gradually add 7 cups water, stirring to loosen particles from bottom of stockpot. Return chicken to stockpot.

2. Combine gravy mix and 1 cup water, stirring well. Add gravy mixture, parsley flakes, and next 10 ingredients to stockpot. Cover and bring to a boil. Reduce heat, and simmer, uncovered, 45 minutes or until slightly thickened, stirring occasionally.

3. Peel shrimp; devein, if desired. Add fish to gumbo mixture; cook 5 minutes. Add shrimp and crabmeat; cook 3 minutes or until shrimp turn pink. Add filé powder; cook 2 minutes, stirring occasionally, or until thickened. Remove and discard bay leaves. Remove gumbo from heat; serve over hot rice. **Makes 22 cups.**

Famous Fried Shrimp

1 lb. unpeeled, jumbo raw wild shrimp (16/20 count)
1 Tbsp. salt
Vegetable oil
1 large egg
1 cup milk
¾ cup self-rising flour

1. Peel shrimp, leaving tails on; devein, if desired.
Combine salt and 3 cups water in a large bowl.
Add shrimp to brine; let stand 20 minutes.
2. Pour oil to a depth of 2 inches into a Dutch
oven; heat over medium-high heat to 375°.
3. Meanwhile, whisk together egg and milk in
a medium bowl. Place flour in a shallow dish.
4. Drain shrimp; pat dry. Dip shrimp in egg
mixture; dredge in flour, shaking off excess. Fry
shrimp, 6 at a time, 2 minutes or until golden
brown. Drain on a wire rack over paper towels.
Makes 3 servings.

Dreamland BBQ

Tuscaloosa, Alabama

Lat./Long. 33.217,-87.5728

5535 15th Avenue E. 35405

(205) 758-8135

www.dreamlandbbq.com

Don't Miss:

Wonder Bread and Sauce

The menu once consisted of only ribs, beer, sauce, and Wonder white bread. That's what you should order when you go. Think of the Wonder bread and tangy sauce sorta like a Deep South version of chips and salsa.

Good barbecue can now even be found in New York City. But great barbecue, being a noun here in the South, comes with some ambiance rules. More to the point, it should be served from a greasy, half-dilapidated shack leaning to starboard. Smoke should be billowing so forcefully that your hair smells like hickory for the next few days. And the place should be filled with characters from a Tennessee Williams play. Dreamland's original location, with its license plate collection, battered furniture, and cheeky "No Farting" sign, makes it a Southern classic. Try to stear clear of knock-off imitations.

Barbecue Pork Quesadillas

½   lb. pulled smoked pork
½   cup barbecue sauce
¼   cup chopped fresh cilantro
4   green onions, finely chopped (about 1 cup)
6   (6-inch) fajita-size flour tortillas
1   cup (4oz.) shredded Mexican four-cheese blend
2   Tbsp. butter, softened
Sour cream

1. Stir together first 4 ingredients.
2. Spoon ⅓ cup pork mixture on half of each of 2 tortillas; sprinkle each with 2 Tbsp. cheese. Fold tortillas in half over filling; spread about 1 tsp. butter on both sides of each quesadilla.
3. Heat a large nonstick skillet over medium heat, and cook quesadillas 2 minutes on each side or until cheese melts. Transfer to a serving plate. Repeat procedure with remaining tortillas, pork mixture, cheese, and butter. Cut each quesadilla into 3 wedges, and serve with sour cream and additional barbecue sauce. **Makes 6 appetizers.**

Dreamland BBQ Brisket

1   (4-lb.) beef brisket, trimmed
1   tsp. lemon pepper
½   tsp. garlic powder
1   (1-oz.) package dried onion soup mix
1   cup baby carrots
1   medium onion, quartered
2½   cups barbecue sauce
Barbecue sauce (optional)

1. Preheat oven to 300°. Rub brisket on all sides with lemon pepper, garlic powder, and onion soup mix. Place brisket in a large Dutch oven. Arrange carrots and onion around brisket. Pour 2½ cups barbecue sauce over beef and vegetables.
2. Cover and bake at 300° for 6 hours, basting occasionally with sauce.
3. Remove from oven, and let brisket stand, uncovered, 20 minutes. Remove from pan, and cut into thin slices. Serve with additional barbecue sauce, if desired. **Makes 8 servings.**
Note: We tested with Dreamland Bar-b-que Sauce.

* Diner Secret: Soup mix adds concentrated flavor during the long slow simmer.

Pie Lab

Greensboro, Alabama

Lat./Long. 32.704075,-87.597419

1317 Main Street 36744

(334) 624-3899

pielab.org

Don't Miss:

Strawberry Lemonade

Pie Lab's delicious concoction, served in an old-fashioned Mason jar, will sweeten your day. It's also a snap to make using frozen strawberries and fresh lemon juice.

Instead of Bunson burners and beakers, you'll find experiments of the delicious sort at Greensboro's most famous eatery. Start your day with their sausage and red pepper quiche, a savory sensation. Fruit pies remain their most popular dishes, however, and they won't disappoint. Pie Lab makes more than just pie—the restaurant also bakes up a healthy community by loaning its space to local charities and not-for-profits.

Apple Pie

1   (14.1-oz.) package refrigerated piecrusts
½   cup of sugar
1   Tbsp. all-purpose flour
1½ tsp. ground cinnamon
Dash of ground nutmeg
5   Granny Smith apples, peeled and cubed
2   Tbsp. lemon juice
1   Tbsp. butter, melted
1   Tbsp. sugar

1. Preheat oven to 400°. Fit 1 piecrust into a 9-inch pie plate according to package directions. Stir together sugar and next 3 ingredients in a large bowl until blended. Add apples. Sprinkle apples with lemon juice, and toss until coated with sugar mixture.

2. Spoon apple filling into prepared crust. Place remaining piecrust over filling; fold edges under, sealing to bottom crust, and crimp. Cut 4 or 5 slits in top of pie for steam to escape. Brush top crust with 1 Tbsp. melted butter, and sprinkle with 1 Tbsp. sugar.

3. Bake at 400° for 5 minutes. Reduce oven temperature to 350°, and bake for 1 hour or until apples are tender and crust is golden. Remove to a wire rack. Cool 1½ to 2 hours before serving. **Makes 8 servings.**

* Diner Secret: A dollop of whipped cream or sour cream is sweet apple pie's perfect pairing.

Peach Pie

¾   cup sugar
¼   cup cornstarch
1   tsp. ground cinnamon
4   cups sliced fresh peaches
1   (14.1-oz.) package refrigerated piecrusts

1. Preheat oven to 350°. Whisk together first 3 ingredients in a saucepan until blended. Add peaches, tossing to coat. Cook, stirring constantly, over medium heat until thick and bubbly. Remove from heat and cool 15 minutes.

2. Meanwhile, unroll piecrusts onto a lightly floured surface; roll out each to a 12-inch circle. Fit 1 piecrust into a 9-inch pie plate. Spoon cooled peach filling into prepared crust. Place remaining piecrust over filling; fold edges under, sealing to bottom crust, and crimp. Cut 4 or 5 slits in top of pie for steam to escape.

3. Bake at 350° for 1 hour. Remove to a wire rack. Cool 2 hours before serving. **Makes 8 servings.**

✳ Diner Secret: Don't forget to let it set! Then slice.

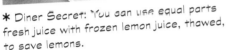

✳ Diner Secret: You can use equal parts fresh juice with frozen lemon juice, thawed, to save lemons.

Strawberry Lemonade

2   cups sugar
1   cup frozen strawberries
2   cups lemon juice
Ice cubes

1. Stir together sugar and 2 cups water in a medium saucepan. Add strawberries, and cook over medium heat until sugar dissolves and strawberries thaw. Remove from heat, and thoroughly mash strawberries with a potato masher.
2. Pour strawberry mixture through a fine sieve into a 1-gal. pitcher; discard solids. Stir in lemon juice and 2 qt. water. Serve immediately over ice, or cover and chill. **Makes 12 servings.**

Pepper Place Farmer's Market

Birmingham, Alabama

There are chefs who know their farmers personally, and then there are the rest. A great meal starts in the dirt, and you'll find that most of the restaurateurs in this book maintain a deep relationship with both their region's farms and farmers. Even the simplest dish is made better by fresh ingredients, grown locally.

In Birmingham, I adore the Pepper Place Saturday Market, which runs (usually) from April through October at the old Dr. Pepper Bottling Co. downtown. Go early. Red ripe tomatoes, okra, green beans, and melons are the staple of just about any market, but what makes Pepper Place special is that you'll also find hand-carved spoons, fresh oatmeal and grits, plants for your garden, and music for your iPod. It's a food scene extraordinaire in the Magic City at 2829 2nd Avenue South.

Food Find:

Alabama

Ezell's Fish Camp

Lavaca, Alabama
Lat./Long. 32.318231,-86.902298

776 Ezell Road 36904

(205) 654-2205

www.ezellsfishcamp.com

Don't Miss:

Frog Legs

If you're a fan of frog legs, you'll find some of the best in the country right here in L.A. (lower Alabama). The batter is light and crispy, making these hoppers addictive.

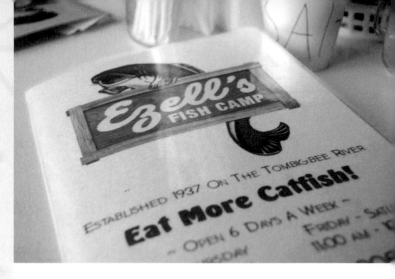

A fish camp should sit right on the river. Fortunately, Ezell's has followed that first commandment of catfish joints, proudly overlooking the banks of the Tombigbee River since 1937. Relax out on the back porch, have a cold beer or some of Janice's sweet (and I mean sweet!) tea, and munch on a basket of fried pickles. Then wait. The best catfish you've ever eaten will soon arrive, tail curled up in a sign of heavenly perfection.

Coleslaw

Serve this sweet slaw with a slotted spoon.

- ½ cup sweet salad cube pickles
- ½ cup mayonnaise
- ¼ cup sugar
- ¼ cup finely minced onion
- ½ tsp. salt
- 1 head cabbage (2¼ lb.), finely shredded (4 cups)

1. Drain pickles in a colander 20 minutes; discard juice.
2. Combine pickles, mayonnaise, and next 3 ingredients in a large bowl; stir well. Gradually add cabbage, stirring well. Cover and chill, if desired. **Makes 4 cups.**

* Diner Secret: This mayonnaise-based slaw has the punch of vinegar thanks to an ample dose of pickles.

Hush Puppies

- 1¼ cups self-rising flour
- 1¼ cups self-rising white cornmeal
- 1 Tbsp. sugar
- ½ tsp. seasoned salt
- ½ tsp. garlic powder
- ¼ tsp. freshly ground pepper
- 1 cup buttermilk
- ½ cup whole kernel corn
- 1 large egg, lightly beaten
- 2½ cups finely chopped onion
- 1 plum tomato, finely chopped

Vegetable oil

* Diner Secret: Keep a can of beer handy. Stir in a little if the hush puppy batter is stiff.

1. Combine first 6 ingredients in a large bowl; stir well. Combine buttermilk, corn, and egg; add to dry ingredients, stirring just until moistened. Stir in onion and tomato.
2. Pour oil to depth of 2 inches into a Dutch oven; heat to 375°. Drop batter by rounded teaspoonfuls, in batches, into hot oil. Fry 2 minutes or until golden, turning once. Drain on a wire rack over paper towels. **Makes 4 dozen.**

Rosie's Cantina

Huntsville, Alabama

Lat./Long. 34.74493,-86.679963

6196 University Drive NW 35806

(256) 922-1001

www.rosiesmexicancantina.com

Don't Miss:

Tres Leches Cake

Never had tres leches cake? Literally translated, it means "three milks"—evaporated milk, condensed milk, and heavy cream. Rosie's version starts with a fluffy sponge cake that doesn't fall apart or lose its firmness. Delicious!

✴ *Diner Secret: Marinating onions cuts their harsh bite and adds zest to these tacos.*

This Rocket City favorite makes the perfect stop if you just happen to be cruising down I-65 and have the taste of Mexico on your mind. You'd have to drive a lot further South to find such authentic flavors. Warning: Don't eat too many of the light, crispy tortilla chips and zippy salsa. You'll want to save room for Rosie's mind-blowing chile relleno, which holds a beefy, cheesy filling that's out of this world.

Mahi-Mahi Fish Tacos

Marinated Onions

1½ cups red wine vinegar

½ cup fresh lemon juice

1½ tsp. salt

1½ tsp. freshly ground pepper

1½ tsp. dried oregano

2 medium-size red onions, thinly sliced

Mahi-Mahi Seasoning

1 tsp. salt

½ tsp. sugar

½ tsp. lemon pepper

½ tsp. ground chipotle chile pepper

½ tsp. paprika

¼ tsp. freshly ground black pepper

Zesty Tartar Sauce

1¼ cups mayonnaise

1 tsp. yellow mustard

2 Tbsp. milk

1 Tbsp. fresh lemon juice

1 Tbsp. finely chopped fresh cilantro

1½ tsp. Mahi-Mahi Seasoning

½ tsp. ground chipotle chile pepper

Mexican Slaw

3½ cups shredded coleslaw mix

¼ cup sugar

¼ cup white vinegar

⅓ cup mayonnaise

1½ tsp. yellow mustard

⅛ tsp. ground red pepper

Tacos

8 (4-oz.) mahi-mahi fillets

2 Tbsp. olive oil

1½ tsp. Mahi-Mahi Seasoning

8 (8-inch) soft taco-size flour tortillas, warmed

1. **Prepare Marinated Onions:** Combine all ingredients; cover and chill 2 to 24 hours.

2. **Prepare Mahi-Mahi Seasoning:** Combine all ingredients in a small bowl; stir well.

3. **Prepare Zesty Tartar Sauce:** Combine all ingredients in a bowl; stir well. Cover and chill 2 hours or until ready to serve.

4. **Prepare Mexican Slaw:** Place coleslaw mix in a medium bowl. Bring sugar and vinegar to a boil in a small saucepan over medium-high heat. Cook 1 to 2 minutes or until sugar dissolves; remove from heat. Drizzle hot vinegar mixture over coleslaw; toss. Stir in mayonnaise, mustard, and red pepper. Cover and chill 2 hours or until ready to serve.

5. **Prepare Tacos:** Brush both sides of fish with oil; sprinkle with seasoning.

6. Preheat grill to 350° to 400° (medium-high) heat. Coat grill rack with cooking spray. Grill fish, covered with grill lid, 5 minutes on each side or until fish flakes with a fork.

7. Break fish into chunks, using a fork, or leave fish in 8 pieces. Place fish in warmed tortillas, and serve with Marinated Onions, Zesty Tartar Sauce, and Mexican Slaw. **Makes 8 servings.**

* Diner Secret: For convenience we used store-bought tortilla strips, but the restaurant fries up different colors each day.

Pollo Santa Fe

Southwestern Sauce

1   cup mayonnaise

½   cup sour cream

3   Tbsp. finely chopped red bell pepper

2   tsp. ground red pepper

1   tsp. garlic powder

1   tsp. paprika

4   tsp. rice vinegar

½   tsp. chili powder

Chicken

6   (8-oz.) skinned and boned chicken breasts

2   Tbsp. olive oil

¼   tsp. salt

¼   tsp. pepper

½   cup (2 oz.) shredded Provolone cheese

2   cups (8 oz.) shredded Monterey Jack cheese

Multicolored tortilla strips

Black Bean–Corn Salsa

1   cup frozen whole kernel corn, thawed

¼   cup finely chopped green bell pepper

¼   cup finely chopped red bell pepper

¼   cup finely chopped red onion

¼   cup coarsely chopped fresh cilantro

¼   cup rice vinegar

2   Tbsp. finely chopped seeded jalapeño pepper

2   Tbsp. olive oil

¾   tsp. salt

¾   tsp. pepper

1   (15-oz.) can black beans, drained and rinsed

1. **Prepare Southwestern Sauce:** Combine all ingredients in a small bowl. Cover sauce and chill 2 hours.

2. **Prepare Chicken:** Preheat grill to 350° to 400° (medium-high) heat. Brush chicken with olive oil, and sprinkle with ¼ tsp. salt and ¼ tsp. pepper. Grill chicken, covered with grill lid, 4 minutes on each side or until done.

3. **Prepare Black Bean–Corn Salsa:** Combine all ingredients in a medium bowl. Cover and chill 2 hours.

4. Preheat oven to 350°. Combine cheeses in a medium bowl. Place chicken breasts on a lightly greased baking sheet. Top each breast with ¼ cup Southwestern Sauce, ¼ cup Black Bean–Corn Salsa, and about ⅓ cup cheese mixture. Bake at 350° for 7 minutes or until cheese melts. Place 1 chicken breast on each of 6 serving plates. Top with tortilla strips. **Makes 6 servings.**

Rubbernecker Wonder:

Huntsville, Alabama

Space Rocket

If you're blasting down I-65, make sure to pull over at the visitor's center as you pass through Elkmont. The modest rest stop is hard to miss, graced with a sleek, towering, 224-foot-tall Saturn 1B (to infinity and beyond!). And it is a fitting welcome as you enter Huntsville, the Rocket City. After you've gotten your outerspace groove on, better make sure to slow down entering Alabama's orbit: The space patrol is always on duty.

Rumor's Deli

Cullman, Alabama

Lat./Long. 34.178434,-86.843802

105 First Avenue 35055

(256) 737-0911

www.rumorsdeli.com

Don't Miss:

Conversation Piece

Chuck your diet entirely and order the "Conversation Piece," a brownie-sized chocolate chip cookie which holds the kind of sweet flavor that will have you talking about Rumor's for years to come.

* Diner Secret: The flavor of a long, slow simmer is achieved with soup mix.

Located in downtown Cullman's hip and historic Warehouse District, Rumor's is full of memorabilia such as a swordfish wearing a Hawaiian shirt, a sled, airplanes, golf clubs, a red wagon, neon signs, and lots of other cool-looking junk. Paper towels grace every table—a considerate feature for a restaurant that serves many tasty, though sloppy, sandwiches such as "The Talk of the Town," a classic Reuben with corned beef on rye bread served with Swiss cheese, sauerkraut, onions, brown mustard, and mayonnaise; and "The Mouth of the South," a killer hoagie loaded with ham, turkey, roast beef, Swiss, smoked Cheddar, and provolone cheese. Finely chopped mushrooms, olives, onions, and green peppers also vie for your taste buds, making the sandwich a well-rounded meal unto itself.

Rumor's Taco Soup

1   lb. ground chuck
1   medium onion, chopped (about 1 cup)
1   (1-oz.) envelope Ranch dressing mix
1   (1-oz.) envelope taco seasoning mix
2   (16-oz.) cans pinto beans, undrained
2   (14.5-oz.) cans diced tomatoes, undrained
1   (15-oz.) can black beans, undrained
1   (14¾-oz.) can white creamed-style corn
1   (4.5-oz.) can chopped green chiles, undrained
Sour cream
Shredded sharp Cheddar cheese
Tortilla chips

1. Cook beef and onion in a large Dutch oven over medium-high heat, stirring often, 10 minutes or until meat crumbles and is no longer pink; drain. Stir in dressing mix and taco seasoning. Add 1 cup water, pinto beans, and next 4 ingredients. Bring to a boil over high heat; reduce heat to medium, and simmer, uncovered, 25 minutes, stirring occasionally.
2. Ladle soup into bowls. Top each serving with a dollop of sour cream, and sprinkle with cheese. Serve with tortilla chips. **Makes 8 servings.**

Miss Isabel's Secret

1   (16-oz.) package refrigerated sugar cookie dough
3   cups powdered sugar
1   cup creamy peanut butter
2   Tbsp. butter, melted
1   cup semisweet chocolate morsels
½   cup butter

1. Preheat oven to 350°. Press cookie dough into bottom and up sides of a lightly greased 9-inch pie plate. Bake at 350° for 40 minutes or until golden. Cool on a wire rack at least 15 minutes.
2. Meanwhile, place 1 cup powdered sugar, peanut butter, ¼ cup water, and 2 Tbsp. melted butter in a large bowl. Beat at medium speed with an electric mixer until smooth. Gradually add remaining 2 cups powdered sugar, beating until moistened. (Mixture will be crumbly.)
3. Firmly press peanut butter mixture into cookie crust.
4. Combine chocolate morsels and ½ cup butter in a medium saucepan. Cook over low heat until chocolate and butter melt, stirring until smooth; pour over peanut butter mixture, spreading to edges of crust. Chill 3 hours or until chocolate is firm. Cut into wedges. **Makes 12 servings.**

* Diner Secret: For perfect wedges, run a knife under hot water, dry it off, then slice.

Chicken Joe Bleu Panini

Caramelized Onion

2   Tbsp. butter
1   large red onion, thinly sliced (1½ cups)
¼   cup balsamic vinegar

White Sauce

1½   cups mayonnaise
½   cup sugar
⅓   cup white vinegar
1   Tbsp. coarsely ground pepper

Panini

4   ciabatta buns, cut in half
¼   cup butter, melted and divided
4   (3- to 4-oz.) chicken breast cutlets
1½   Tbsp. taco seasoning mix
¾   cup (3 oz.) crumbled blue cheese
1   cup spring greens mix

1. **Prepare Caramelized Onion:** Melt 2 Tbsp. butter in a medium skillet over medium heat. Add onion; cook 13 minutes or until tender and beginning to brown, stirring occasionally. Stir in balsamic vinegar; reduce heat to low, and cook, uncovered, 26 minutes or until onion is golden brown, stirring occasionally.

2. **Meanwhile, prepare White Sauce:** Stir together all ingredients in a medium bowl until smooth.

3. **Prepare Paninis:** Brush cut sides of buns with 2 Tbsp. melted butter. Cook ciabatta bun halves in batches in a preheated panini press 2 minutes or until toasted.

4. Sprinkle cutlets with taco seasoning. Cook cutlets, in batches, in panini press 5 minutes or until done. Cut cutlets in half.

5. Spread 1 Tbsp. White Sauce on cut side of each bun half. Layer each bun bottom with a cutlet half, 2 Tbsp. Caramelized Onion, 3 Tbsp. cheese, ¼ cup greens, and a bun top. Brush tops of sandwiches with remaining 2 Tbsp. melted butter. Cook sandwiches in panini press 2 minutes or until golden brown. **Makes 4 servings.**

Rubbernecker Wonder:

Birmingham, Alabama

Vulcan

The second-largest statue in the United States, Vulcan stands high over Birmingham atop Red Mountain. This god of iron enthralls visitors with his huge hands, commanding brow, and naked bum, which is why locals say there's a permanent full moon over Alabama's most populous city.

These are buns of iron not buns of steel.

Look!

Greetings From ARKANSAS

State Capital in Little Rock

State Flower the Apple Blossom

eka Springs 'S • ECHO

Arkansas

Best Drive

Hot Water in Hot Springs

The state spreads out before you like a lush green quilt when you motor the Talimena Scenic Drive. You'll meander down Arkansas 88 from Mena, Arkansas, and wind up in Talihina, Oklahoma (hence "Talimena"). The drive takes you over the 2,681-foot Rich Mountain and through the 1.8 million-acre Ouachita National Forest, which spans from central Arkansas into southeastern Oklahoma. The forest offers recreational opportunities for everyone, from hiking and mountain biking to hunting and fishing. Visit the US Forest Service website for information at www.fs.fed.us. **Length:** 54 miles

Arkansas

Big John's Shake Shack

Marion, Arkansas

GPS COORDINATES:
Lat./Long. 35.211566,-90.189982

409 Military Road 72364
(870) 739-3943

Don't Miss:

Peanut Brittle

Good Southern peanut brittle, the kind that snaps brightly with your first chomp and develops a rich, filling-pulling chew as you eat it, has become a rarity in today's fast-food world. Owner Loretta Tacker's brittle is worth the stop. Her humidity-fighting secret: Put it near an air-conditioning vent to cool, then bag it immediately.

I f Elvis were still piloting a Cadillac around the Delta, Big John's Shake Shack would undoubtedly be one of the King's favorite haunts. Not only does Big John's celebrate Mr. Presley, but the restaurant's also filled with other American movie legends and mid-century memorabilia. The hamburgers, fries, and super-thick shakes seem straight out of the fifties too. Families love the laid-back feel, and so will you.

Caramel Apple

Apple

Loretta's Bread Pudding

2   cups milk
1½   cups sugar
½   cup butter, melted
1   tsp. vanilla extract
4   large eggs
5   French bread slices, cut into 1-inch cubes (5 cups)
1   Tbsp. sugar
1   tsp. ground cinnamon

1. Preheat oven to 350°. Whisk together first 5 ingredients in a large bowl. Arrange bread cubes in a lightly greased 2-qt. baking dish. Pour egg mixture over bread, pressing gently with a spoon to soak bread.

2. Combine 1 Tbsp. sugar and cinnamon; stir well. Sprinkle cinnamon-sugar mixture over bread pudding. Bake at 350° for 55 minutes or until set and golden brown. **Makes 6 to 8 servings.**

Charlotte's Eats & Sweets

Keo, Arkansas

GPS COORDINATES:
Lat./Long. 34.543204,-91.968761

290 Main Street 72083

(501) 842-2123

Don't Miss:

Coconut Pie

The meringue atop one of Charlotte Bowl's coconut pies stands almost as tall as a 5-pound bag of sugar. If coconut's not your thing, there are plenty more choices.

Charlotte mixes fresh coconut into a mountain of meringue and then adds even more coconut filling to her skyscraping pie. But the Arkansas pie master doesn't limit her baked concoctions just to coconut; she also makes a dozen other varieties from caramel to chocolate.

For the past 16 years, Charlotte has used recipes gathered from her family and friends. Now she teaches those recipes to her granddaughter, Michaela Coffey, who has joined her in the family business. You will thank your lucky tastebuds that this pie perfection is being passed down.

Chocolate Pie

A favorite—velvety chocolate pudding nestled between sweet, golden meringue and a tender, flaky crust.

Pastry

1   cup all-purpose flour
½   tsp. salt
⅓   cup shortening
3   to 4 Tbsp. ice water

Chocolate Filling

1   cup sugar
¼   cup plus 1 tsp. cornstarch
¼   cup unsweetened cocoa
¼   tsp. salt
1½ cups milk
½   cup evaporated milk
4   extra-large egg yolks, beaten
2   Tbsp. butter
2   Tbsp. vanilla extract

Meringue

4   extra large egg whites
¼   tsp. cream of tartar
¼   cup sugar

1. Prepare Pastry: Preheat oven to 450°. Stir together flour and ½ tsp. salt in a large bowl. Cut shortening into flour mixture with a pastry blender until mixture resembles small peas. Mound mixture on 1 side of bowl.

2. Drizzle 1 Tbsp. ice water along edge of mixture in bowl. Using a fork, gently toss a small amount of flour mixture into water just until dry ingredients are moistened; move mixture to other side of bowl. Repeat procedure with remaining ice water and flour mixture.

3. Gently gather dough into a flat disk on a floured work surface. Roll out pastry to ⅛-inch thickness. Fit pastry into a 9-inch pie plate; trim off excess pastry along edges. Fold edges under, and crimp. Prick bottom and sides of pastry with a fork. Bake at 450° for 9 minutes or until golden brown. Set pastry aside on a wire rack while preparing filling. Reduce oven temperature to 325°.

4. Prepare Chocolate Filling: Combine sugar and next 3 ingredients in a medium saucepan. Gradually stir in milks. Cook, stirring constantly, over medium-high heat until mixture comes to a boil; boil, stirring constantly, 1 minute. Remove from heat. Gradually stir about one-fourth of hot milk mixture into yolks; add yolk mixture to remaining hot milk mixture, stirring constantly. Cook, stirring constantly, over medium heat 3 minutes. Remove from heat; add butter and vanilla, stirring until butter melts. Cover and keep warm.

5. Prepare Meringue: Beat egg whites and cream of tartar at high speed with an electric mixer until foamy. Gradually add sugar, 1 Tbsp. at a time, beating until stiff peaks form and sugar dissolves. Pour hot filling into pastry. Spread meringue over hot filling, sealing edges.

6. Bake at 325° for 20 minutes or until golden. Cool completely on a wire rack. **Makes 8 servings.**

Caramel (Burnt Sugar) Pie

Charlotte uses a Crisco-based crust. When making the recipe on the Crisco can, never add extra flour! It'll be tough.

Pastry

1	cup all-purpose flour
½	tsp. salt
⅓	cup shortening
3	to 4 Tbsp. ice water

Caramel Filling

1¼	cups sugar, divided
2	Tbsp. all-purpose flour
1½	Tbsp. cornstarch
⅛	tsp. salt
½	cup milk
1	(12-oz.) can evaporated milk
4	extra-large egg yolks, beaten
2	Tbsp. butter
2	Tbsp. vanilla extract

Meringue

4	extra-large egg whites
¼	tsp. cream of tartar
¼	cup sugar

1. **Prepare Pastry:** Preheat oven to 450°. Stir together flour and ½ tsp. salt in a large bowl. Cut shortening into flour mixture with a pastry blender until mixture resembles small peas. Mound mixture on 1 side of bowl.

2. Drizzle 1 Tbsp. ice water along edge of mixture in bowl. Using a fork, gently toss a small amount of flour mixture into water just until dry ingredients are moistened; move mixture to other side of bowl. Repeat procedure with remaining ice water and flour mixture.

3. Gently gather dough into a flat disk on a floured work surface. Roll out pastry to ⅛-inch thickness. Fit pastry into a 9-inch pie plate; trim off excess pastry along edges. Fold edges under, and crimp. Prick bottom and sides of pastry with a fork. Bake at 450° for 9 minutes or until golden brown. Set pastry aside on a wire rack while preparing filling. Reduce oven temperature to 325°.

4. **Prepare Caramel Filling:** Combine 1 cup sugar and next 3 ingredients in a medium saucepan. Gradually stir in milks. Cook, stirring constantly, over medium-high heat until mixture comes to a boil; boil, stirring constantly, 1 minute or until thickened. Remove from heat. Gradually stir about one-fourth of hot milk mixture into yolks; add yolk mixture to remaining hot milk mixture, stirring constantly. Cook, stirring constantly, over medium-low heat 3 minutes. Remove from heat; add butter and vanilla, stirring until butter melts. Cover and keep warm.

5. Sprinkle remaining ¼ cup sugar in a 1-qt. heavy saucepan; place over medium heat and cook, shaking pan constantly, until sugar melts and turns a light golden brown. Remove from heat. Carefully stir custard mixture into caramelized sugar until blended. Cover and keep warm.

6. **Prepare Meringue:** Beat egg whites and cream of tartar at high speed with an electric mixer until foamy. Gradually add sugar, 1 Tbsp. at a time, beating until stiff peaks form and sugar dissolves. Pour hot filling into pastry. Spread meringue over hot filling, sealing edges.

7. Bake at 325° for 25 minutes or until golden. Cool completely on a wire rack. **Makes 8 servings.**

Colonial Pancake House

Hot Springs, Arkansas

GPS COORDINATES:
Lat./Long. 34.51875,-93.055784

111 Central Avenue 71901

(501) 624-9273

Don't Miss:

Stuffed French Toast

The stuffed French toast at the Colonial Pancake House comes in a variety of flavors: apricot, apple, strawberry, blueberry, or peach. Their delicious recipe, featured here, lends itself to fruit fillings, but you might also experiment with chocolate chips or even crumbled sausage.

For breakfast, brunch, and yes, "brinner," Colonial Pancake House serves up the perfect meal. Made-from-scratch pancakes, waffles, and French toast are best ordered alongside their rich omelettes, ham steaks, and farm-fresh eggs. Bottomless cups of coffee and fresh orange juice served in a Mason jar seal the deal. Colonial Pancake House remains a Hot Springs institution, loved by generations of breakfast-goers. Try it once, and you'll be hooked too.

Colonial Stuffed French Toast

8   large eggs
1   Tbsp. sugar
2   tsp. ground cinnamon
2   tsp. vanilla extract
Pinch of salt
1   (8-oz.) package cream cheese, softened
⅓   cup maple syrup
8   Texas toast slices
2   Tbsp. butter
1   (21-oz.) can cherry pie filling
Sweetened whipped cream
Toasted walnuts

1. Whisk eggs in a shallow dish. Whisk in sugar and next 3 ingredients. Combine cream cheese with maple syrup in another bowl. Beat at medium speed with an electric mixer until creamy.
2. Dip toast slices in egg mixture 10 seconds on each side. Melt butter on a large griddle over medium heat. Cook toast slices 2 to 3 minutes on each side or until golden.
3. Place 4 toast slices on each of 4 serving plates. Top each slice with 2 Tbsp. cream cheese mixture and ¼ cup pie filling. Top with remaining toast slices. Dollop with sweetened whipped cream, and sprinkle with walnuts. Serve immediately. **Makes 4 servings.**

You'll feel victorious after devouring this mountain of pie filling and cream.

Daniel Boone and I discuss our favorite syrups and French toast toppings.

Ray's Dairy Maid

Barton, Arkansas

GPS COORDINATES:
Lat./Long. 35.43422,-97.407804

5322 Highway 49 72312
(870) 572-3060

Don't Miss:
Cream Pie

When asked for her pie wisdom, Deane Cavette laughs and says simply, "I like them sweet." These pies will cure any sugar craving. The coconut pecan can be made a few days ahead and keeps well. Deane's cream pie recipe is best eaten the day you make it.

Southerners love pie. And here in the Delta, just across the river from Tunica, pie-lovers can feast on some of the best. For 50 years, owner Deane Cavette has made her restaurant guests happy. Her pecan-coconut pie (page 43) will really make you smile. The unique flavor blend of coconuts, pecans, and creamy buttermilk may sound unusual, but the result will be an instant favorite at family gatherings.

Coconut Cream Pie

½ (14.1-oz.) package refrigerated piecrusts
1 cup sugar, divided
¼ cup cornstarch
⅛ tsp. salt
2 cups milk
3 large eggs, separated
1 cup sweetened flaked coconut
¼ cup butter
1 tsp. vanilla extract
½ tsp. cream of tartar
Dash of salt

1. Preheat oven to 450°. Roll piecrust into a 13-inch circle on a lightly floured surface. Fit into a 9-inch pie plate; fold edges under, and crimp. Prick bottom and sides of piecrust with a fork. Bake at 450° for 10 minutes or until piecrust turns golden brown. Reduce oven temperature to 350°.
2. Combine ¾ cup sugar, cornstarch, and ⅛ tsp. salt in a heavy saucepan; gradually whisk in milk and egg yolks. Bring to a boil over medium heat, whisking constantly; continue to boil, whisking constantly, 3 minutes. Remove from heat.
3. Stir in coconut, butter, and vanilla. Cover tightly with plastic wrap.
4. Beat egg whites, cream of tartar, and salt at high speed with an electric mixer until foamy. Gradually add ¼ cup sugar, 1 Tbsp. at a time, beating until stiff peaks form and sugar dissolves. Spoon hot filling into baked piecrust. Spread meringue over hot filling, sealing edges. Bake at 350° for 10 to 12 minutes or until golden brown. Remove from oven to a wire rack, and cool completely (4 hours). **Makes 8 servings.**

Nana Deane's Pecan-Coconut Pie

½ (14.1-oz.) package refrigerated piecrusts
3 large eggs
2 cups sugar
½ cup buttermilk
¼ cup butter, melted and cooled
2 Tbsp. all-purpose flour
1 tsp. vanilla extract
Dash of salt
¾ cup chopped pecans
½ cup sweetened flaked coconut

1. Preheat oven to 350°. Roll piecrust into a 13-inch circle on a lightly floured surface. Fit into a 9-inch pie plate; fold edges under, and crimp.
2. Whisk together eggs and next 6 ingredients until thoroughly blended. Stir in pecans and coconut. Pour mixture into piecrust.
3. Bake at 350° on lowest oven rack 50 minutes or until pie is set. Cool on a wire rack 2 hours or until completely cool. **Makes 8 servings.**

* Diner Secret: This decadent pie is a combination of two Southern favorites—buttermilk pie and pecan pie.

Ed & Kay's

Benton, Arkansas

GPS COORDINATES:
Lat./Long. 34.564527,-92.603805302
15228 I-30N 72019
(501) 315-3663

Don't Miss:

The Pie

Hands down, it's the biggest reason folks park it in a booth at Ed & Kay's. Take your pick of pies. You won't be disppointed.

I believe one can divide the world into cookie/cake/pastry people and pudding/pie/custard people. My heart lies with the pie. The South is full of pie, ranging from chocolate to pecan. One pie towers above the others: the meringue pie. When it comes to meringue, nobody piles it higher than Ed & Kay's. Famous for their PCP (pineapple, coconut, and pecan) pie, Ed & Kay's also serves chocolate, lemon, and coconut meringue.

PCP Pie (Pineapple-Coconut-Pecan Pie)

½ (14.1-oz.) package refrigerated piecrusts
4 large eggs
2 cups sugar
½ cup butter, melted
1 Tbsp. yellow cornmeal
1 Tbsp. all-purpose flour
1 tsp. vanilla extract
1 cup chopped pecans
1 cup sweetened flaked coconut
1 (20-oz.) can crushed pineapple, drained
Garnish: sweetened flaked coconut

1. Preheat oven to 350°. Unroll piecrust. Fit into a 9½-inch deep-dish pie plate; fold under edges of crust, and crimp.
2. Whisk eggs in a large bowl until lightly beaten. Whisk in sugar and next 4 ingredients until blended. Stir in pecans and next 2 ingredients. Pour filling into prepared crust.
3. Bake at 350° for 50 to 60 minutes or until pie filling is almost set in center, shielding loosely with aluminum foil, if necessary. Remove to a wire rack; cool completely. Garnish, if desired. **Makes 8 servings.**

The best part about this sign? It's spelled wrong. However you spell it, it's worth a chuckle.

Rubbernecker Wonder:

Greasy Corner, Arkansas

If you're heading east on I-40, a few miles outside of Memphis at the junction of Highway 149, you'll see this priceless, misspelled sign for "Greasey Corner."

Signs are awesome. And in this day of GPS, smart phones, and digital mapping, they still play an essential role in navigation. If, like me, you're a collector of funny town names, Arkansas won't disappoint. In addition to Greasy Corner, you'll find Hogeye, Snowball, Romance, Smackover, and my favorite, Toad Suck. If you can't stop laughing, stop in a Tom's Nut House and they'll fix you up.

Greetings From DELAWARE

State Capital in Dover

State Flow...
the Peach Blos...

Since 1927, Dolle's Salt Water Taffy has been a favorite stop in Rehoboth Beach.

Delaware

Best Drive

Route 9 Coastal Heritage Scenic Byway

With a nickname like "The First State," it would be rude not to explore a little of Delaware's history while you're here. The most historic spot on this route has to be New Castle, which is just south of Wilmington. It's the real deal when it comes to Colonial America. Nearby seaport towns Delaware City and Port Penn were developed by the C&D Canal and have any number of enchanting historic homes and businesses to explore. In addition to the many significant towns you'll see on Route 9, don't miss the Bombay Hook National Wildlife Refuge and the John Dickinson Plantation just shy of the end of the drive. **Length:** 52 miles

Krazy Kat's

Wilmington, Delaware

Lat./Long. 39.790071,-75.589464

528 Montchanin Road 19710

(302) 888-4200

www.krazykatsrestaurant.com

Don't Miss:

French Toast

The French toast on the weekends is a treat that will make you want to stay another week.

The Inn at Montchanin Village gives every appearance of a high-end, stuffy experience. And make no mistake, it's not cheap. But stuffy? No. A visit to the inn's restaurant, Krazy Kat's, will dispel any thought that the place is pretentious. The hilarious portraits of dogs and cats that grace the walls of the main dining room are outdone only by the superior food, wine list, and service. The superb menu features such delights as pan-seared foie gras in a port wine reduction and a bread pudding dessert topped with ice cream that, in the words of one waiter, "will make you want to jump up and slap somebody!"

Vanilla-Cognac-Brined Pork Tenderloin

½   cup cognac

¼   cup sugar

3   Tbsp. kosher salt

1   Tbsp. chopped fresh thyme

1   Tbsp. chopped fresh rosemary

1   Tbsp. chopped fresh sage

1   Tbsp. vanilla extract

1½   tsp. fennel seeds

1½   tsp. coriander seeds

1½   tsp. black peppercorns

2   bay leaves

1   vanilla bean, split lengthwise

4   (¾-lb.) pork tenderloins

Gingersnap Jus

1. Combine first 12 ingredients and 3½ cups water in a bowl; stir well. Remove silver skin from pork tenderloins, leaving a thin layer of fat. Place 1 (2-gal.) zip-top plastic freezer bag inside another 2-gal. zip-top plastic freezer bag. Place tenderloins in the inside bag; pour cognac brining mixture over tenderloins. Seal both bags, and chill 24 hours, turning occasionally. (Double bagging is a precaution to avoid spills.)
2. Preheat grill to 350° to 400° (medium-high) heat. Remove tenderloins from bag; discard brine. Pat tenderloins dry with paper towels.
3. Grill tenderloins, covered with grill lid, 12 minutes on each side or until a meat thermometer inserted in thickest portion registers 155°. Remove from grill; let pork stand 10 minutes. Cut pork diagonally into slices, and arrange on a serving platter. Serve with Gingersnap Jus. **Makes 12 to 14 servings.**

* Diner Secret: Completely submerge the pork in this vanilla-flavored brine for maximum flavor impact.

Gingersnap Jus

18   gingersnap cookies

1½   tsp. olive oil

¼   cup diced onion

½   tsp. caraway seeds

½   cup Burgundy wine

2   Tbsp. red wine vinegar

4   cups beef broth

2   Tbsp. molasses

1. Pulse cookies in a food processor 25 times or until finely ground; set aside.
2. Heat oil in a medium saucepan over medium-high heat. Sauté diced onion and caraway seeds 2 minutes or until onion is tender. Add wine and vinegar, stirring to loosen particles from bottom of saucepan. Add broth, reduce heat to medium, and simmer 20 minutes. Slowly whisk in molasses and reserved cookie crumbs, stirring until blended and thickened, about 1 minute. Remove from heat. Serve with Vanilla-Cognac-Brined Pork Tenderloin. **Makes 5 cups.**

Sweet Somethings

Wilmington, Delaware

GPS COORDINATES:

Lat./Long. 39.75452,-75.569082

1006 North Union Street 19805

(302) 655-7211

www.sweetsomethingsdesserts.com

Don't Miss:

Anything Chocolate

Whether it's dark, milk or white, the chocolate desserts at Sweet Somethings are showstoppers well worth the indulgence.

You can't get a whole meal here, but you can certainly order my favorite part— dessert. This traditional bakery whips up an unbelievable assortment of last courses for many of the best restaurants in town. Their chocolate silk torte is as smooth as a Beltway politico. The mini cheesecake feels like it weighs 30 pounds. Tartes, toffees, and tortes will keep you dreaming of sugar for weeks to come.

Chocolate Silk Torte

Cake

- 1   (18.25-oz.) package devil's food cake mix
- 3   large eggs
- ½   cup vegetable oil
- 4   oz. white chocolate, chopped
- 1   cup heavy cream
- 20   chocolate wafers

Ganache

- ¾   cup heavy cream
- 6   Tbsp. milk
- 2   cups semisweet chocolate morsels

Filling

- 2   (8-oz.) packages cream cheese
- 1⅓   cups sugar

1. **Prepare Cake:** Preheat oven to 350°. Combine cake mix, eggs, oil, and 1⅓ cups water in a large bowl. Beat at low speed with an electric mixer 30 seconds. Beat at medium speed 2 minutes. Pour batter into 3 greased and floured 8-inch round cake pans. Bake at 350° for 16 minutes or until a wooden pick inserted in center comes out clean. Cool in pans on wire racks 10 minutes; remove from pans to wire racks, and cool completely (about 30 minutes).

2. **Meanwhile, prepare Ganache:** Bring ¾ cup cream and milk to a simmer in a heavy saucepan over medium heat. Remove from heat; add chocolate morsels, stirring until melted. Divide Ganache into 1¾-cup and ½-cup portions. Cover each portion and chill.

3. **Prepare Filling:** Beat cream cheese and 1⅓ cups sugar at medium speed with an electric mixer until fluffy. Add 1¾ cups Ganache, beating at low speed until smooth. Reserve ⅓ cup Filling.

4. Place 1 cake layer in bottom of an 8-inch springform pan. Spread half of remaining Filling on top of cake layer in pan. Top with a second cake layer. Spread remaining half of Filling over second cake layer. Top with third cake layer. Cover and freeze 8 hours.

5. Place chopped white chocolate in a 6-oz. custard cup. Microwave at HIGH 30 seconds or until chocolate melts, stirring every 10 seconds. Freeze chocolate 30 minutes or until hardened. Remove chocolate from freezer; dip bottom of custard cup in hot water for about 45 seconds. Unmold chocolate onto a small, wax paper–lined plate. Chill white chocolate disk until firm. Shave white chocolate into curls using a vegetable peeler. Chill until ready to use.

6. Remove chilled cake from freezer; let stand 5 minutes. Unwrap and remove sides of pan. Transfer cake to a cake plate. Spread reserved ⅓ cup Filling in a thin layer on all sides of cake. Beat 1 cup heavy cream until soft peaks form. Spread whipped cream on top and sides of cake.

7. Process chocolate wafers in a food processor until fine crumbs form. Carefully pat crumbs on sides of cake.

8. Microwave ½ cup Ganache at HIGH 40 seconds or just until pourable, stirring every 10 seconds. Drizzle warm Ganache over cake, and top with white chocolate curls. Store finished cake in refrigerator. **Makes 10 to 12 servings.**

Note: We tested with Duncan Hines Moist Deluxe Devil's Food Cake Mix.

White Chocolate Banana Cream Pie with Sugar Cookie Crust

Sugar Cookie Crust

½ cup all-purpose flour

1 (16.5-oz.) package refrigerated sugar cookie dough

White Chocolate Shavings

4 oz. white chocolate, coarsely chopped

White Chocolate Banana Cream Filling

½ cup sugar

3½ Tbsp. cornstarch

⅛ tsp. salt

2 cups milk

4 large eggs

¼ cup butter, cut into small pieces

4 oz. white chocolate, chopped

1 tsp. vanilla extract

2 Tbsp. lemon juice

4 small bananas

Toppings: 1 cup whipping cream, whipped; unsweetened cocoa

This dessert tastes even more awesome than it looks!

1. **Prepare Sugar Cookie Crust:** Knead flour into cookie dough. Roll out dough to ⅛-inch thickness on a lightly floured surface. Fit dough into a 9½-inch tart pan with removable bottom; press into fluted edges, and trim excess. Prick bottom of dough with a fork. Freeze pie crust for 30 minutes.

2. **Meanwhile, prepare White Chocolate Shavings:** Place chopped white chocolate in a 6-oz. custard cup. Microwave at HIGH 30 seconds or until chocolate melts, stirring every 10 seconds. Freeze chocolate 30 minutes or until hardened. Remove chocolate from freezer; dip bottom of custard cup in hot water for about 45 seconds. Unmold chocolate onto a small wax paper–lined plate. Chill chocolate disk until firm. Shave chocolate into curls using a vegetable peeler. Chill until ready to use.

3. Preheat oven to 350°. Bake crust for 15 minutes or until golden brown. Carefully pat crust down (it will puff when baked). Cool crust completely in pan on a wire rack.

4. **Meanwhile, prepare White Chocolate Banana Cream Filling:** Combine first 3 ingredients in a medium saucepan. Gradually whisk in milk. Cook over medium heat, stirring constantly, until thickened and bubbly. Beat eggs until foamy. Gradually stir about one-fourth of hot mixture into eggs; add to remaining hot mixture, stirring constantly. Cook over medium heat, stirring gently, 3 minutes. Remove from heat; add butter and white chocolate, stirring until melted. Stir in vanilla. Set aside.

5. Stir together 1 qt. water and lemon juice in a 2-quart bowl. Cut bananas into ½-inch-thick

slices; place in cold water mixture for 30 seconds, stirring gently to coat slices. Drain well.

6. Arrange banana slices in a single layer in bottom of cooled crust. Pour warm custard over bananas, spreading to edges of crust. Place heavy-duty plastic wrap directly on warm filling (to prevent a film from forming); chill 2 hours. (Mixture will thicken as it cools.)

7. Remove plastic wrap from filling, and top with whipped cream, spreading to within ½ inch of edge of tart. Sprinkle with White Chocolate Shavings, and dust with cocoa. **Makes 8 servings.**

Throughout the South, farmers offer up the bounty of the region.

Delaware's Roadside Stands

From seaside stalls to inland booths, Delaware's rich soil provides homegrown bounty worth braking for.

Go early: The best produce is often found right at the opening of the market.

Go often: Buy only as much produce as you will use within a few days, and store it in the refrigerator or a cool, dark area. Flavor, vitamins, and nutrients diminish over time.

Bright is best: Always look for blemish-free, brightly colored fruits and vegetables. Any damaged areas will spoil quicker.

Don't wash right away: Wash your produce just before cooking or serving—not before storing

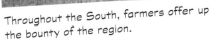

Delaware

Greetings from FLORIDA

The Home of
KEY WEST
ORIGINAL
CONCH FRITTERS

KEYLIME ICE TEA · LEMON LIME SURPRISE

Key West is called "The Conch Republic," a name coined on April 23, 1982, the city's unofficial "Independence Day."

Florida

Best Drive

The Highway That Goes to Sea

Tourists who fly from Miami to Key West miss the Overseas Highway or the southernmost leg of Highway 1, perhaps one of the most amazing drives in the world. It's a road that takes visitors over 42 bridges spanning blue-green water and lush nature sanctuaries. Originally built in 1912 as Henry Flagler's Florida East Coast Railroad, the highway took shape during the Great Depression. Don't miss the Grassy Key Bikeway, added in 2002, which may rank as the most perfect spot to catch a sunrise or sunset in the South. **Length:** 113 miles

Blue Heaven

Key West, Florida

GPS COORDINATES:

Lat./Long. 24.551744,-81.802836

729 Thomas St. 33040

(305) 296-8666

www.blueheavenkw.com

Don't Miss:

Roosters and Coconuts

The first, like most of Key West, will surprise you, and the second might just knock you silly.

Breakfast in a storied building that once housed a bordello, pool hall, cockfighting arena, and Ernest Hemingway has some good mojo behind it. Blue Heaven attracts all the weirdo, off-beat, out-of-kilter stuff that makes Key West so much fun. Plus they make a mean banana bread, homemade granola, and eggs Benedict. Their brilliant mimosa or spicy breakfast Bloody Mary will take the stinger out of whatever stung you on the cruise ship.

BLUE HEAVEN

Serving heaven on a fork and sin in a glass.

Shrimp and Grits

1⅓ cups half-and-half

1½ tsp. salt

1⅓ cups uncooked quick-cooking grits

1½ cups (6 oz.) shredded sharp white Cheddar cheese

1½ lb. unpeeled large raw shrimp (21/25 count)

¾ cup butter

½ cup dry white wine

½ cup chopped green onions

Cracked pepper

Garnish: additional shredded sharp white Cheddar cheese

1. Bring 4 cups water, half-and-half, and salt to a boil in a large saucepan. Gradually stir in grits. Reduce heat, and simmer over medium-low heat 7 minutes or until thickened. Remove from heat. Stir in 1½ cups cheese. Cover and keep warm.
2. Peel shrimp; devein, if desired. Melt butter in a large skillet over medium-high heat; add wine.

✶ Diner Secret: Use very ripe bananas for the best banana flavor.

Bring to a boil; boil 2 minutes. Add shrimp; cook 2 minutes or until shrimp turn pink. Stir in chopped green onions; cook, stirring constantly, 30 seconds. Remove from heat.
3. Spoon cheese grits into 4 serving bowls; spoon shrimp mixture over grits. Sprinkle with cracked pepper. Garnish, if desired. **Makes 4 servings.**

Banana Bread

½ cup butter, softened

1 cup sugar

2 large eggs

1 cup mashed ripe bananas

¼ cup sour cream

1 tsp. vanilla extract

1½ cups sifted all-purpose flour

1 tsp. baking soda

¼ tsp. salt

1. Preheat oven to 350°. Beat butter at medium speed with an electric mixer until fluffy; gradually add sugar, beating well. Add eggs, 1 at a time, beating until blended after each addition.
2. Combine bananas, sour cream, and vanilla. Combine flour, baking soda, and salt in another bowl; add to butter mixture alternately with banana mixture, beginning and ending with flour mixture. Beat at low speed until blended after each addition, stopping to scrape bowl as needed. Pour batter into a greased 9- x 5-inch loaf pan.
3. Bake at 350° for 1 hour or until a wooden pick inserted in center comes out clean. Cool in pan on a wire rack 10 minutes; remove from pan to a wire rack, and cool 30 minutes before slicing. **Makes 1 loaf.**

Island Cow

Sanibel Island, Florida
GPS COORDINATES:
Lat./Long. 26.436855, -82.071603

2163 Periwinkle Way 33957
(239) 472-0606
www.sanibelislandcow.com

Don't Miss:

Olde Fashion Egg Cream

It's like stepping back in time. (If you've not had one, it's essentially a chocolate soda.) The other drinks not to miss on the menu are the frozen smoothies. They come in a variety of tropical flavors (from mango to piña colada) and are topped with whipped cream.

Sanibel Island is my best-kept secret for a romantic stateside escape. While it feels like you've ventured down to the Bahamas or Bermuda, this tiny Gulf island is just a short Southwest Airlines flight for most Southerners. Island Cow is the perfect first stop to get yourself in sync with island time. Have a chocolatey egg cream or scarf down a basket of conch and shrimp fritters. Sit outside on the "thrones of the lawn" to read the day's paper, sip your toddy, or simply enjoy some rest and relaxation under the Florida sunshine.

Island Granola

Oats, nuts, and berries provide healthful fiber, omega-3s, and antioxidants for breakfast or a snack.

3   cups regular oats
1   cup walnut halves
1   cup sliced almonds
¾   cup sweetened flaked coconut
½   cup honey
¼   cup extra virgin olive oil
1   Tbsp. vanilla extract
1   cup dried cranberries
Powdered sugar
Sliced strawberries and blueberries
Cold milk

1. Preheat oven to 250°. Toss together first 4 ingredients in a large bowl. Stir together honey, olive oil, and vanilla in a separate bowl. Drizzle honey mixture over oat mixture, tossing until coated. Spread half of oat mixture in each of 2 lightly greased 15- x 10-inch jelly-roll pans.
2. Bake at 250° for 1 hour and 15 minutes or until toasted, stirring every 15 minutes. Remove from oven. Cool completely in pans on wire racks.
3. Transfer granola to a large airtight container. Add cranberries; toss well. Store covered.
4. To serve, spoon granola into large shallow bowls. Dust granola with powdered sugar, and serve with fresh berries and cold milk. **Makes 10 servings.**

Boiled Peanuts

From Florida to Virginia

If you are Southern-impaired, you may not know the divine pleasure of a boiled peanut. But Southerners—from diamond-wearing dowagers to face-painted football fans—love this damp, salty snack with a passion. Best way to try them? From a black-iron cauldron in a lopsided shack by the side of the road. If it looks sanitary keep driving.

Food Find:

Stinky's Fish Camp

Santa Rosa Beach, Florida

GPS COORDINATES:

Lat./Long. 30.355665,-86.096432

5960 Highway 30-A 32459

(850) 267-3053

www.stinkysfishcamp.com

Don't Miss:

Stinky's Stew

Unlike some restaurant soups, which are made in multi-gallon batches, Stinky's Stew was designed from the get-go as a single serving. Chock-full of seafood, this made-to-order bowl of goodness is just what the doctor ordered.

Nothing stanks at Stinky's. Let's just get that straight. Okay, maybe the live bait they sell stinks a tad, but the food is divine. In fact, this phenomenal spot on the Panhandle rivals any white-tablecloth restaurant I've ever tried. The crawfish pie's rich and flakey crust hides a buttery goodness you'll want to lick. The "oyster log" is a Stinky's invention that needs to catch on across America—one can never have too many delicious roasted and fried oysters.

* Diner Secret: Add a splash of white wine for flavor and a crumbling of crackers for texture.

Mee Maw's Crab Po'Boy

We used authentic bread from New Orleans. French bread or sub rolls may be substituted.

- ¼ cup butter
- ¾ cup chopped onion
- ¾ cup chopped celery
- 2 Tbsp. white wine
- 1 Tbsp. fresh lemon juice
- ½ tsp. salt
- ½ tsp. pepper
- ⅛ tsp. hot sauce
- 1 lb. fresh lump crabmeat, drained
- 7 round buttery crackers, crushed
- 2 Tbsp. chopped fresh parsley
- 2 green onions, chopped
- 3 (7-inch) po'boy rolls or 3 French bread rolls or sub rolls

1. Melt butter in a large skillet over medium-high heat. Add onion and celery; sauté 5 minutes or until tender. Add wine; bring to a simmer. Stir in lemon juice and next 3 ingredients. Stir in crabmeat; toss gently. Stir in crushed crackers, parsley, and green onions. Cook 1 minute. Remove from heat.

2. Split rolls. Spread bottoms evenly with crabmeat filling. Cover with roll tops. Cut rolls in half.

3. Cook sandwiches, in batches, in a preheated panini press 2 minutes or until golden brown. Makes 6 servings.

Think fast or you'll end up in the ocean!

Crawfish Pie

Stinky's bakes and serves this rich seafood pie in small bowls.

4½   cups chicken broth
½   cup butter
1½   cups chopped onion
1   cup chopped celery
½   cup chopped red or green bell pepper
1½   Tbsp. minced garlic
½   cup all-purpose flour
1½   tsp. Old Bay seasoning
1½   tsp. minced canned chipotle pepper in adobo sauce
½   tsp. jarred chicken soup base
½   tsp. jarred seafood soup base
¼   tsp. freshly ground pepper
1   bay leaf
1   (1-lb.) package frozen cooked peeled and deveined crawfish tails, thawed
½   (10-oz.) can diced tomatoes and green chiles
1   (8-oz.) package pepper Jack cheese, diced
2   green onions, sliced
Pie Dough
1   large egg, lightly beaten

1. Bring broth to a simmer in a large saucepan over medium heat. Meanwhile, melt butter in a large Dutch oven over medium-high heat. Add onion and next 2 ingredients; sauté 6 to 7 minutes or until tender. Add minced garlic; sauté 1 minute. Add flour; cook, stirring constantly, 10 minutes or until browned.

2. Add simmering broth, 1½ cups at a time, to sautéed mixture; whisk until blended. Add Old Bay seasoning and next 5 ingredients, whisking until blended. Bring to a boil; reduce heat to low, and simmer, uncovered, 20 minutes.

3. Stir crawfish tails, tomatoes, and green chiles into mixture; cook 1 minute or just until thoroughly heated. Remove from heat; stir in cheese and green onions.

4. Preheat oven to 425°. Turn out pie dough onto a lightly floured surface. Roll each dough to ⅛-inch thickness. Cut out 8 circles, each large enough to cover top of a 10-oz. ramekin. Lightly grease 8 (10-oz.) ramekins. Spoon about 1 cup crawfish pie filling into each ramekin; top with dough cutouts, and crimp, sealing to ramekins. Brush tops with beaten egg. Cut slits in top for steam to escape.

5. Place ramekins on an aluminum foil–lined baking sheet. Bake at 425° for 25 to 30 minutes or until browned and bubbly. **Makes 8 servings.**

Pie Dough

Make and chill this basic pie dough in advance, if desired.

3   cups all-purpose flour
1   tsp. salt
1   cup butter, cut into pieces
10   Tbsp. ice-cold water

1. Combine flour and salt in a large bowl, stirring well. Cut butter into flour mixture with a pastry blender until mixture resembles small peas. Sprinkle ice-cold water, 1 Tbsp. at a time, over surface of mixture in bowl; stir with a fork until dry ingredients are moistened.

2. Shape dough into 2 flat disks. Wrap disks in plastic wrap, and chill 1 to 24 hours. **Makes 2 dough disks.**

Whitey's Fish Camp

Orange Park, Florida
Lat./Long. 30.101031,-81.745068

2032 County Road 220 32003
(904) 269-4198
www.whiteysfishcamp.com

Thursday Nights

That's when local fishermen return from a few hours on the lake with their bounty for a weigh-in. The winner takes home a pot that can reach up to $1,000. Grab a seat at the Tiki bar for the best view (and sounds) of the action.

The bona fides of a fish camp: Pickup truck parking. Check. Bass boat docking. Check. Bait for sale. Check. Fried catfish that will make you want to jump up and down and holler. Check. It all comes together to make Whitey's the casual dining treasure of this Navy town. Outstanding fresh (and local) catfish, a veritable brewery of cold beers on tap, and creative dishes such as Red Snapper Siena, featured on page XX, will keep you coming back for more.

Crab and Shrimp Cakes

1½ cups Japanese breadcrumbs (panko)
1 cup chopped green onions
1 cup mayonnaise
½ cup cracker meal
½ cup chopped red onion
¼ cup chopped red bell pepper
¼ cup chopped green bell pepper
1 tsp. salt
1 tsp. pepper
1 tsp. Old Bay seasoning
1 tsp. minced garlic
2 lb. fresh lump crabmeat, drained
10 oz. peeled, small cooked shrimp (36/45 count)
Wax paper
2½ cups olive oil

1. Stir together first 11 ingredients in a large bowl. Pick crabmeat, removing any bits of shell. Chop shrimp. Fold crabmeat and shrimp into breadcrumb mixture. Shape crabmeat mixture into 10 (¾-inch-thick) cakes; place on a baking sheet lined with wax paper. Cover and chill at least 2 hours or overnight.

2. Fry crab cakes, in 3 batches, in hot oil in a large skillet over medium-high heat 2 to 3 minutes on each side or until golden brown and warmed through. Drain on a wire rack over paper towels. **Makes 10 servings.**

*Diner Secret: A quick sear is all that's needed to help detach the skin from the fish.

Red Snapper Siena

1¼   cups butter, divided
¼   cup minced onion
¼   cup minced garlic
½   cup dry white wine
¼   cup fresh lemon juice
1   (8.5-oz.) jar sun-dried tomatoes in oil,
     drained and chopped
6   Tbsp. chopped fresh basil
¼   cup drained capers
¾   tsp. kosher salt, divided
¾   tsp. ground white pepper, divided
6   (7-oz.) red snapper fillets, skin on
⅔   cup (2.7 oz.) shredded mozzarella cheese

1. Preheat oven to 425°. Melt ¼ cup butter in a medium saucepan over medium heat. Add onion and garlic; sauté 7 minutes or until tender. (Do not brown.) Increase heat to medium-high. Stir in wine and lemon juice. Bring to a boil; boil, uncovered, 8 minutes or until reduced by half.
2. Meanwhile, cut remaining 1 cup butter into small pieces. Reduce heat to low. Add butter, a few pieces at time, whisking until butter melts. Stir in tomatoes, next 2 ingredients, ½ tsp. salt, and ½ tsp. white pepper. Remove from heat.
3. Heat a large nonstick skillet over high heat; coat pan with cooking spray. Add fish, skin side down, in 3 batches, to pan. Cook 30 seconds; carefully remove fish from skin, and place in 2 lightly greased 13- x 9-inch baking dishes. Sprinkle fish evenly with remaining ¼ tsp. salt and remaining ¼ tsp. white pepper. Top fish with sauce; sprinkle with cheese.
4. Bake, uncovered, at 425° for 17 minutes or until fish flakes with a fork. **Makes 6 servings.**

Rubbernecker Wonder:

Pensacola, Florida

The UFO House

Those of you who have a fear of waking up in a zero-gravity operating room with your short-term memory wiped out might avoid Pensacola Beach. My rocket-finned Cadillac felt right at home with the Futuro house, a prefab saucer designed by Matti Suuronen and built, along with dozens of others across the world, in the 1960s and 1970s. Made from fiberglass and plastic, this one has survived multiple hurricanes and storms.

Look!

Greetings from GEORGIA

State Capital in Atlanta

State Flower
the Cherokee Rose

R-B-Q
COL. POOLE'S
Pig Hill of Fame

Col. Poole's "hill of fame" in East Ellijay features a mass of plywood pigs, each painted with the name of a customer.

SELLERS ORC

Georgia

Best Drive

Blairsville to Helen

Visit Blairsville and you'll understand why so many Scots chose to settle in the rolling hills of North Georgia. It looks like the Scottish Highlands, especially in June when the area goes positively plaid for the Scottish Festival and Highland Games. You'll have to put the hammer down to get up Brasstown Bald, which peaks at 4,784 feet above sea level. The summit gives commanding vistas of Georgia, Tennessee, and North and South Carolina. End your adventure in Helen, which is a re-creation of an Alpine village. Funnel cakes and schnitzel await, and in the fall, visitors enjoy the longest Oktoberfest in the South.

Length: 43 miles

Antica Posta

Atlanta, Georgia

GPS COORDINATES:

Lat./Long. 33.839488,-84.369171

519 East Paces Ferry Road 30305

(404) 262-7112

www.anticaposta.com

Don't Miss:

Panna Cotta

The sublimely simple panna cotta is served with fresh berries.

Big-city dining can intimidate, and many visitors to Atlanta feel overwhelmed by the vast number of dining choices to be found. Go to Buckhead. Yes, posh and upscale Buckhead. There, you'll find Antica Posta, a modest yellow house where authentic Tuscan plates of arugula and rabbit, beef carpaccio, handmade pastas, and fresh fish come flying out of the small, unpretentious kitchen. With dishes starting at $9, you can't go wrong with dinner in this tiny cottage.

Panna Cotta con Salsa ai Frutti di Bosco

2   envelopes unflavored gelatin
1   cup cold water
4   cups heavy cream
⅔   cup sugar
1   Tbsp. vanilla extract
Wild Berry Sauce
Garnishes: fresh raspberries, fresh mint leaves

1. Sprinkle gelatin over cold water in a small saucepan; let stand 1 minute. Cook over low heat, stirring until gelatin dissolves (about 2 minutes). Bring heavy cream and sugar to a simmer in a medium saucepan over medium heat, stirring constantly. Cook, stirring constantly, until sugar dissolves. Remove pan from heat; stir in gelatin and vanilla.
2. Pour mixture into 10 (6-oz.) custard cups. Cover and chill 8 to 24 hours.
3. To unmold, run a knife between panna cottas and sides of custard cups to loosen. Immerse cups, 1 at a time, in hot water halfway up sides of cups until edges of dessert soften (about 15 seconds). Invert each dessert onto a plate, gently removing cup using small knife to release dessert. Drizzle each dessert with Wild Berry Sauce. Garnish, if desired. **Makes 10 servings.**

Wild Berry Sauce

1½   cups fresh raspberries
1   cup red wine
2   Tbsp. sugar

1. Bring all ingredients to a boil in a small saucepan over medium-high heat. Reduce heat, and simmer 10 minutes. Remove from heat; cool. Process in a food processor or blender until smooth, stopping to scrape down sides as needed. Cover and chill until ready to serve. **Makes 1¼ cups.**

✳ Diner Secret: Spiking the berry sauce with red wine elevates this simple Italian classic to highfalutin indulgence.

The masters of the meal at Antica Posta

Georgia

72

✱ *Diner Secret: Green chile adds kick to this elegant pasta dish.*

Farfalle All' Aragosta

Bow-tie pasta, white wine, and fresh Maine lobster mingle in this succulent entrée.

8 oz. farfalle (bow-tie) pasta
1 Anaheim pepper, halved and seeded
3 Tbsp. extra virgin olive oil, divided
1 cup chopped green onions
¾ cup seeded, diced tomato
2 large garlic cloves, chopped
¼ cup lobster stock
½ tsp. salt
¼ tsp. freshly ground pepper
¾ cup chopped cooked lobster
2 Tbsp. chopped fresh parsley

1. Cook pasta according to package directions, except cooking 2 minutes less than package suggests. Chop half of seeded Anaheim pepper; reserve remaining half for another use.
2. Heat 2 Tbsp. oil in a large nonstick skillet over medium-high heat. Add green onions, tomato, garlic, and chopped Anaheim pepper; sauté 1 minute. Add lobster stock, salt, pepper, and cooked pasta. Cook 1½ minutes, stirring constantly. Add lobster meat; cook 1 minute or until thoroughly heated. Remove from heat; drizzle with remaining 1 Tbsp. oil, and sprinkle with parsley. **Makes 2 servings.**
Note: We tested with 2 (8-oz.) lobster tails and asked our friends at the fish market to steam them for us.

Rubbernecker Wonder:

Rome, Georgia

Capitoline Wolf Statue

Visit both Rome, Italy, and this Georgia town and you'll find the Capitoline Wolf statue. The bronze masterpiece represents the legend of Romulus and Remus, twins raised by a she-wolf after the overthrow of their father. Oddly, the statue was a gift to Rome, Georgia, from Benito Mussolini, a dictator who apparently not only made the trains run on time but also had an affection for wolf statues. Go figure.

Look!

B. Matthew's Eatery

Savannah, Georgia

GPS COORDINATES:

Lat./Long. 32.07991,-81.087547

325 East Bay Street 31401

(912) 233-1319

www.bmatthewseatery.com

Don't Miss:

Dessert

The desserts will leave you reeling. Choose from gorgeous baked pies, cookies, cakes, and the biggest, fluffiest wagon-wheel of a cinnamon roll you'll find in Georgia.

Sometimes a worn-around-the-edges vibe really works for a bakery. B. Matthews' vintage feel and sassy staff combine to make the ideal spot to relax for an afternoon. The black-eyed pea cake sandwich is one of the South's more unusual dishes and comes on a fantastic slab of bread. The bacon, cherry tomato, and blue cheese pasta salad "blue" me away. And even a simple smoked-turkey sandwich with Cheddar and green apples made the perfect lunchtime meal unto itself.

Pancakes with Apple-Walnut-Bourbon Chutney

2   cups unbleached all-purpose flour
2½   Tbsp. sugar
1½   tsp. baking powder
1   tsp. baking soda
3   egg yolks
1½   cups buttermilk
1¼   cups heavy cream
2   Tbsp. butter, melted
1   tsp. vanilla extract
Apple-Walnut-Bourbon Chutney

Bourbon makes everything better!

1. Combine first 4 ingredients in a large bowl. Whisk together egg yolks and next 4 ingredients in a medium bowl. Add egg mixture to flour mixture, whisking until blended.

2. Pour about ½ cup batter for each pancake onto a hot buttered griddle or large nonstick skillet. Cook 2 minutes or until tops are covered with bubbles and edges look dry and cooked; turn and cook 2 minutes or until golden brown. Place pancakes in a single layer on a baking sheet, and keep warm in a 200° oven up to 30 minutes. Top pancakes with chutney. **Makes 12 pancakes.**

Apple-Walnut-Bourbon Chutney

¼   cup butter
4   Golden Delicious apples, peeled, cored, and diced (6 cups)
¼   cup firmly packed light brown sugar
¼   cup bourbon
1   cup walnuts, coarsely chopped and toasted

1. Melt butter in a large nonstick skillet over medium-high heat. Add apples; sauté 5 minutes or

A trolley car weaves you through the streets of Savannah, uncovering secrets along the way.

until apples begin to brown. Reduce heat to low; cover and cook 15 minutes, stirring occasionally. Uncover skillet; increase heat to medium, and stir in brown sugar and bourbon. Cook 1 minute. Remove from heat; stir in walnuts. Serve warm or at room temperature. **Makes 2½ cups.**

Black-eyed Pea Cakes with Cajun Rémoulade

Cajun Rémoulade

1	cup mayonnaise
¼	cup chopped green onions
1½	tsp. fresh lemon juice
1½	tsp. capers, drained
1	small clove garlic, minced
½	tsp. hot sauce
½	tsp. refrigerated horseradish
¼	tsp. salt
¼	tsp. pepper
½	jarred roasted red bell pepper

Dash of ground red pepper

Black-Eyed Pea Cakes

1	Tbsp. canola oil
½	cup chopped onion
½	cup chopped red bell pepper
¼	cup chopped fresh cilantro
1	tsp. ground cumin
2	(15.8-oz.) cans black-eyed peas, drained and rinsed
1	tsp. salt
½	tsp. freshly ground pepper
1	cup dry breadcrumbs
⅓	cup canola oil

Serve these versatile pea cakes as a hearty appetizer or on buns as flavorful veggie burgers.

Work up an appetite and get a nap waiting at sea turtle crossings.

1. **Prepare Cajun Rémoulade:** Process all ingredients in a food processor 2 minutes or until smooth. Cover and chill until ready to serve.
2. **Prepare Black-Eyed Pea Cakes:** Heat 1 Tbsp. oil in a large skillet over medium-high heat. Add onion and bell pepper; sauté 3 minutes or until tender. Add cilantro and cumin; sauté 1 more minute. Remove from heat, and let cool slightly.
3. Process black-eyed peas, onion mixture, salt, and pepper in a food processor until smooth. Spoon mixture into a bowl; stir in breadcrumbs. Shape mixture into 10 (2-inch) cakes.
4. Heat ⅓ cup canola oil over medium heat in a large nonstick skillet. Fry patties, in 2 batches, 2 minutes on each side or until crisp and golden brown. Drain on paper towels. Serve with Cajun Rémoulade. **Makes 10 servings.**

White Chocolate Banana Bread French Toast

White Chocolate Banana Bread

½   cup butter, softened

1⅓   cups sugar

4   large eggs

2   cups mashed bananas (about 4 bananas)

¼   cup heavy cream

2   tsp. vanilla extract

2   tsp. fresh lemon juice

1   tsp. almond extract

3   cups all-purpose flour

2   tsp. baking powder

1   tsp. baking soda

1   tsp. salt

1½   tsp. ground cinnamon

1   cup white chocolate morsels

Custard

8   large eggs

1   Tbsp. vanilla extract

1½   tsp. ground cinnamon

1   tsp. ground nutmeg

2   cups heavy cream

6   Tbsp. butter

Maple syrup

1. Prepare White Chocolate Banana Bread: Preheat oven to 350°. Beat butter at medium speed with an electric mixer until creamy; gradually add sugar, beating well. Add eggs, 1 at a time, beating until blended after each addition.

2. Stir together bananas and next 4 ingredients in a bowl. Mix flour and next 4 ingredients in another bowl; add to butter mixture alternately with banana mixture, beginning and ending with flour mixture. Beat at low speed until blended after each addition, stopping to scrape sides of bowl as needed. Fold in white chocolate morsels. Pour batter into 2 lightly greased 8⅓- x 4½-inch loaf pans.

3. Bake at 350° for 1 hour or until a wooden pick inserted in center comes out clean. Cool in pans on wire racks 10 minutes; remove from pans to wire racks, and cool completely (about 30 minutes).

4. Prepare Custard: Whisk first 4 ingredients in a bowl. Whisk in cream. Cut each banana bread loaf into 12 slices. Dip 4 banana bread slices in custard 2 minutes on each side. Melt 1 Tbsp. butter on a griddle over medium heat. Add coated slices to pan. Cook 2 minutes on each side or until golden. Remove to a serving platter; keep warm. Repeat procedure 3 more times with remaining slices, custard, and butter. Serve toast with maple syrup. **Makes 12 servings.**

Fenders Diner

Cornelia, Georgia

GPS COORDINATES:
Lat./Long. 34.51134,-83.527859

631 Irvin Street 30531

706-776-2181

www.fendersrestaurant.com

Don't
Miss:

The Shakes

Though Fenders opened in 1996, it gives off a vibe of a time when gas was 20 cents a gallon and a Chevy cost $2,000. The menu is standard diner fare, but the shakes will knock your bobby socks off. My advice? Have a malted version.

On Saturday nights in Cornelia, Georgia, you may think you've slipped back in time. Blue-and-pink leatherette booths host malt-sipping folks inside Fenders Diner. Outside on the street, gleaming muscle cars invite gawking and oohing. Whether you roll into town driving a finned '59 Caddy or a fine new minivan, you'll discover a fun small town for both dining and shopping.

No matter what day of the week you arrive, pop in to Fenders for an old-fashioned chocolate milk shake, a Big Bopper burger, and some crispy fries. Decorated to look like a malt shop from the fifties, Fenders welcomes cruise-ins on the first Saturday evening of the month. Monday through Friday, the diner adds home-style options—such as fried chicken and macaroni and cheese—to the menu.

Hummingbird Cake

3   cups all-purpose flour, sifted
2   cups sugar
1   tsp. salt
1   tsp. baking soda
1   tsp. ground cinnamon
1½   cups vegetable oil
1½   tsp. vanilla extract
3   large eggs, lightly beaten
1⅔   cups ripe bananas, mashed
2   cups chopped pecans, divided
1   (8-oz.) can crushed pineapple, undrained
2   (8-oz.) packages cream cheese, softened
1   cup butter, softened
2   (16-oz.) packages powdered sugar
2   tsp. vanilla extract

1. Preheat oven to 350°. Combine first 5 ingredients in a large bowl; add oil, 1½ tsp. vanilla, and eggs, stirring just until dry ingredients are moistened. (Do not beat.) Stir in bananas, 1 cup pecans, and pineapple.

2. Pour batter into 3 greased and floured 9-inch round cake pans. Bake at 350° for 25 minutes or until a wooden pick inserted in center comes out clean. Cool in pans on wire racks 10 minutes; remove from pans, and cool completely on wire racks.

3. When cake is cool, beat cream cheese and butter at medium speed with an electric mixer until creamy. Gradually add powdered sugar, beating until light and fluffy. Stir in 2 tsp. vanilla extract and remaining 1 cup pecans.

4. Spread frosting between layers and on top and sides of cooled cake. Store cake in refrigerator. **Makes 16 servings.**

Watergate Salad

Mix it up by substituting other pudding flavors.

1   (20-oz.) can crushed pineapple in juice, undrained
1   (3-oz.) package pistachio instant pudding
1½   cups frozen whipped topping, thawed
1   cup miniature marshmallows
½   cup chopped pecans

Garnish: Pecan halves

1. Stir together pineapple and pudding in a medium serving bowl until blended. Fold in whipped topping and next 2 ingredients. Cover and chill 1 hour. Garnish, if desired. **Makes 8 to 10 servings.**

✱ Diner Secret: Fenders' retro recipes conjure memories of church suppers and grandma's kitchen.

✳ Diner Secret: Evaporated milk provides richness in this classic mac.

Oven-Baked Mac-n-Cheese

1   (16-oz.) package elbow macaroni
3   Tbsp. butter
3   Tbsp. all-purpose flour
1   (12-oz.) can evaporated milk
1   tsp. salt
1   tsp. pepper
5   cups (20 oz.) shredded Cheddar cheese, divided

1. Preheat oven to 425°. Cook pasta according to package directions, omitting salt and fat; drain. Place pasta in a lightly greased 13- x 9-inch baking dish.

2. Melt butter in a heavy saucepan over low heat; whisk in flour until smooth. Cook 1 minute, whisking constantly. Gradually whisk in milk, 1½ cups water, salt, and pepper; cook over medium heat, whisking constantly, 18 minutes or until mixture begins to thicken.

3. Add 4 cups cheese; stir until cheese melts and sauce thickens. Pour cheese sauce evenly over pasta; sprinkle with remaining 1 cup cheese.

4. Bake, uncovered, at 425° for 15 minutes or until golden. **Makes 12 to 15 servings.**

Sweet Grass Dairy

Thomasville, Georgia

The delicious handcrafted farmstead cheeses produced from the milk of the goats and Jersey cows grazing on the property of this tiny artisanal dairy can be purchased on site or found in area markets. They take Internet orders too! Try their Georgia Pecan Chévre with dried fruit and a glass of chilled Sauvignon Blanc. Go to www.sweetgrassdairy.com to order, or pick some up in person at the dairy: 19635 US Highway 19 North.

Food Find:

Georgia

GREETINGS FROM KENTUCKY

State Capital in Frankfort

State Flower the Goldenrod

SLEEP IN A WIGWAM

Ya' never know what sort of adventures you'll find when driving through the South.

Kentucky

Best Drive

Bourbon Trail

The French have Champagne. The Scots have their smoky whisky. Kentucky has Bourbon. The region is full of gorgeous tree-lined roads, stunning horse farms, and, on this golden trail, six distilleries (Four Roses, Heaven Hill, Jim Beam, Maker's Mark, Wild Turkey, and Woodford Reserve). There are plenty of other Kentucky icons to visit while you're tooling around the Bluegrass. Just don't try to drink and drive the route. **Length:** approximately 150 miles

Kentucky

The Brown Hotel

Louisville, Kentucky

GPS COORDINATES:

Lat./Long. 38.250697,-85.831159

335 West Broadway 40202
(502) 583-1234
www.brownhotel.com

Don't Miss:

Mint Julep

The Gilded-Age elegance of The Brown's lobby and bar creates the perfect place to relax after a long day on the road. Order a mint julep and a Hot Brown, and park it in one of the comfy sofas to people-watch.

A lot of hotels these days may only be good for a free breakfast buffet. But The Brown, as befits its long heritage of excellence, serves up the best example of two of Kentucky's greatest dishes. First, The Brown's classic mint julep defies tradition with a long, tall glass, which cuts the sweet of this venerable cocktail. As a result, you'll be tempted to have more than one. If you drink more than three, I recommend The Brown's other famous tradition: the Hot Brown. Its renowned combination of turkey, tomato, butter, cream, cheese, and bacon will cure any hangover.

Crab Cakes with Tomato Relish and Basil Oil

Crab Cakes

1	lb. fresh jumbo lump crabmeat, drained
1	(8-oz.) French bread loaf, crust removed and torn into pieces
1	Tbsp. Dijon mustard
1½	tsp. Worcestershire sauce
¼	tsp. salt
¼	tsp. pepper
1	large egg
¾	cup heavy cream, whipped
¼	cup vegetable oil

Basil Oil

| 2 | cups packed fresh basil leaves |
| 1 | cup vegetable oil |

Tomato Relish

2	Tbsp. finely chopped fresh rosemary
2	Tbsp. extra virgin olive oil
¼	tsp. salt
¼	tsp. pepper
1½	cups quartered cherry tomatoes
⅓	cup finely diced red onion
½	cup watercress

✱ Diner Secret: Whipped cream makes these crab cakes extra tender.

1. **Prepare Crab Cakes:** Pick crabmeat, removing any bits of shell. Process bread pieces in a food processor to measure 3 cups fine breadcrumbs.

2. Combine mustard and next 4 ingredients in a medium bowl, beating with a fork until blended. Gently stir in crabmeat and breadcrumbs, leaving some lumps of crabmeat. Fold in whipped cream; cover and chill 4 hours.

3. **Meanwhile, prepare Basil Oil:** Cook basil in boiling water to cover 10 seconds. Drain and rinse with cold water; drain. Pat basil dry with paper towels. Process basil and 1 cup oil in a blender or food processor until smooth. Pour basil mixture through a strainer into a bowl; discard solids. Cover and chill until ready to serve.

4. **Prepare Tomato Relish:** Stir together first 4 ingredients in a medium bowl. Add tomatoes and onion, tossing to coat; cover and chill. Add watercress just before serving; toss gently.

5. Preheat oven to 375°. Shape crab mixture into 10 (3-inch) patties, using about ⅓ cup crab mixture for each patty. Heat 2 Tbsp. oil in a large nonstick skillet over medium-high heat. Add 5 patties, and cook 2 minutes on each side or until golden; drain on paper towels. Repeat procedure with remaining crab mixture and 2 Tbsp. oil.

6. Place crab cakes on a baking sheet coated with cooking spray. Bake at 375° for 8 minutes or until golden brown. Serve immediately with Tomato Relish; drizzle with Basil Oil. **Makes 5 servings.**

✱ Diner Secret: A luscious sauce and bacon topping
have made this turkey sandwich famous.

The Hot Brown

Make this classic sandwich with left-over holiday roasted turkey for best flavor.

¼ cup butter

⅓ cup all-purpose flour

4 cups heavy cream

10 Tbsp. grated pecorino Romano cheese, divided

¼ tsp. salt

½ tsp. pepper

1 lb. thinly sliced roasted turkey breast

4 Texas toast slices

4 plum tomatoes, halved lengthwise

¼ tsp. paprika

8 cooked bacon slices

2 Tbsp. chopped fresh parsley

1. Preheat broiler with oven rack 4 inches from heat. Melt butter in a heavy 2-qt. saucepan over medium-low heat; whisk in flour until smooth. Cook 2 minutes, whisking constantly. Gradually whisk in cream; cook over medium heat, whisking constantly, 3 minutes until mixture is thickened and bubbly. Stir in ½ cup cheese, salt, and pepper.

2. Trim crusts from toast. Place 1 toast slice in each of 4 (24-oz.) lightly greased individual casserole dishes. Place 2 tomato halves beside each toast slice. Top toast slices with turkey. Spoon cheese sauce over turkey and tomato; sprinkle with remaining 2 Tbsp. cheese.

3. Broil 5 minutes or until cheese begins to brown. Sprinkle with paprika. Arrange 2 bacon slices in an "X" pattern on top of each casserole. Sprinkle with parsley. **Makes 4 servings.**

Rubbernecker Wonder:

Louisville, Kentucky

World's Largest Baseball Bat

The Louisville Slugger, a bat that most every American child has swung, is made right downtown. To commemorate the American icon, the factory built a 120-foot version that replicates the wooden bat Babe Ruth used in the Roaring Twenties. You can't miss it on the Louisville skyline, as it actually stands taller than the factory itself. Make sure to take a tour of the Louisville Slugger Museum while you're there.

As American as apple pie, this museum celebrates our favorite pastime.

Look!

Lynn's Paradise Cafe

Louisville, Kentucky

Lat./Long. 38.236759,-85.728651

984 Barret Avenue 40204

(502) 583-3447

www.lynnsparadisecafe.com

Don't Miss:

BLT Hash Browns

The BLT ranks among the world's best sandwiches, and in typical fashion Lynn's Paradise Cafe has figured out how to make the classic Southern favorite a little bit better: Combine it with potatoes. Manager Patti Schnotter jokingly calls it, "a heart attack in a bowl." You'll call it divine.

Wacky. Eclectic. A bizarre bazaar. It all started with an ugly lamp competition judged by six bachelors—those guys know ugly. Today, the ever-fun Lynn's Paradise Cafe remains festooned with everything from tomato hats to teabag trousers. The decor may be bonkers (we love it), but the food is nothing short of stupendous. Breakfast specialities such as Bourbon Ball French Toast and fresh-squeezed mimosas will delight. Lynn's is truly a roadside paradise.

BLT Hash Browns

Vegetable cooking spray
- 1 (20-oz.) package refrigerated shredded hash browns
- 1 tsp. salt
- 1 tsp. pepper
- 1 cup chopped red onion
- 4 cups packed fresh baby spinach, thinly sliced
- 1 cup diced tomato
- 2 cups (8 oz.) shredded Monterey Jack Cheese
- 12 bacon slices, cooked and crumbled

Horseradish Sour Cream (optional)

1. Preheat oven to 400°. Heat a large nonstick skillet over medium-high heat. Coat pan with cooking spray. Add potatoes; sprinkle with the salt and pepper, and coat with cooking spray. Cook potatoes, uncovered, 10 minutes or until browned and crisp, stirring occasionally.

2. Heat another nonstick skillet over medium-high heat. Coat pan with cooking spray. Add onion, and sauté 3 minutes. Divide potatoes into 4 portions. Place portions on a large rimmed baking sheet coated with cooking spray. Layer onion, spinach, tomato, and cheese evenly over potato portions. Bake at 400° for 15 minutes or until heated and cheese melts. Sprinkle with bacon. Serve immediately with Horseradish Sour Cream, if desired. **Makes 4 servings.**

Horseradish Sour Cream

- ½ cup sour cream
- 1 Tbsp. refrigerated horseradish
- ¼ tsp. salt
- ¼ tsp. pepper

1. Stir together all ingredients in a small bowl. **Makes ½ cup.**

Look for Ronald McDonald moonlighting with his mandolin on the weekends.

This is paradise, where everything is served with a smile.

...and the fork ran away with the spoon.

* Diner Secret: Spiked with bourbon and a hint of maple syrup, this cream sauce takes humble fried chicken over the top.

Pecan Chicken in Woodford Reserve Maple Cream Sauce

Pecan Chicken

6   skinned and boned chicken breasts

1   cup buttermilk

Vegetable oil

1   cup pecan halves

2   cups all-purpose flour

2   Tbsp. kosher salt

Woodford Reserve Maple Cream Sauce

4   peppered bacon slices

¼   cup minced shallots

3   Tbsp. all-purpose flour

½   cup maple syrup

⅓   cup whole grain Creole mustard

⅓   cup bourbon

1   tsp. Dijon mustard

½   tsp. kosher salt

2   cups heavy cream

1. **Prepare Pecan Chicken:** Place chicken and buttermilk in a large zip-top plastic freezer bag. Seal and chill 8 hours.

2. Pour oil to a depth of 1 inch into a large deep skillet; heat over medium-high heat to 350°.

3. Meanwhile, process pecans in a food processor until very finely chopped. Transfer pecans to a bowl; stir in 2 cups flour and 2 Tbsp. kosher salt.

4. Remove chicken from buttermilk, discarding buttermilk. Dredge in flour mixture, 2 pieces at a time, shaking off excess; fry chicken, in 2 batches, 6 to 7 minutes on each side or until done. Drain on a wire rack over paper towels. Keep warm.

5. **Prepare Woodford Reserve Maple Cream Sauce:** Cook bacon in a large saucepan over medium heat 10 minutes or until crisp; remove bacon, and drain on paper towels, reserving drippings in pan. Crumble bacon; add shallots to drippings; sauté 2 minutes or until tender. Stir in 3 Tbsp. flour; cook, stirring constantly, over medium heat 2 minutes or until lightly browned. Stir in syrup and next 4 ingredients. Cook, stirring constantly, 3 more minutes or until thick. Stir in cream. Bring to a simmer over medium heat; cook, stirring constantly, 5 to 8 minutes or until thickened. Serve chicken with sauce and bacon. **Makes 6 servings.**

Rebecca Ruth Candy

Frankfort, Kentucky

Have dessert at the famous Rebecca Ruth Candy Factory on Second Street. The store, founded by two school teachers in 1919, has an interesting history and satisfying line of chocolates laced with Kentucky liquors. Tempt yourself with their online catalog at www.rebeccaruth.com.

Farm Boy Restaurant

Morgantown, Kentucky

Lat./Long. 37.230872,-86.691964

607 West GL Smith Street 42261

(270) 526-4649

Don't Miss:
Fried Oreos

An Oreo becomes fluffy, but more to the point, irresistible, when one fries it. There, I said it.

Love and a deep fryer seem to be the two key ingredients in just about every dish on this family restaurant's menu. Fried catfish, country-fried steak, French fries, fried hushpuppies, fried chicken, fried ice cream, and even fried Oreos won't please your cardiologist, but you'll leave with a smile. Opened by A.C. Phelps (the original farm boy) in 1968, it's a family affair. On any given night, you may be served by one of the farm boy's children or grandchildren.

Farm Boy Southern-Style Meatloaf

2½ lb. ground chuck
1¼ cups finely chopped onions
¾ cup finely chopped green bell pepper
2 large eggs
1 (1.5-oz.) envelope meatloaf seasoning
1 sleeve saltine crackers, crushed
1½ cups ketchup, divided

1. Preheat oven to 350°. Combine first 6 ingredients and ½ cup ketchup in a large bowl, using hands. Shape mixture into a 12- x 6-inch loaf; place on a lightly greased rack in a broiler pan lined with aluminum foil.
2. Bake at 350° for 1 hour and 15 minutes. Spread remaining 1 cup ketchup over meatloaf. Bake 15 more minutes or until no longer pink in center. Let meatloaf stand 10 minutes before serving. **Makes 10 to 12 servings.**

I dare you to share a slice of this pie. It'll wreck a relationship.

Peanut Butter Crunch Pie

Peanut butter streusel hides under the cream filling and graces the top of this pie, making it a multi-layered mix of creamy and crunchy heaven.

1 (9-inch) frozen unbaked deep-dish piecrust shell
1 cup powdered sugar
½ cup chunky peanut butter
2 cups milk
½ cup sugar
3½ Tbsp. cornstarch
⅛ tsp. salt
4 egg yolks
¼ cup butter, cut into pieces
1 tsp. vanilla extract

1. Preheat oven to 400°. Bake piecrust shell according to package directions. Cool completely on a wire rack.
2. Stir together powdered sugar and peanut butter until crumbly. Sprinkle ½ cup peanut butter crumb mixture into prepared piecrust; reserve remaining crumb mixture for top.
3. Whisk together milk and next 4 ingredients in a heavy saucepan. Bring to a boil over medium heat, whisking constantly. Boil, whisking constantly, 3 minutes or until thickened. Remove pan from heat; gently whisk in butter and vanilla until smooth.
4. Pour warm filling over crumb mixture in piecrust. Sprinkle with remaining reserved crumb mixture. Cover and chill 4 to 8 hours. **Makes 8 servings.**

Woodford Reserve Distillery

Versailles, Kentucky

Lat./Long. 38.115674,-84.81071

7855 McCracken Pike 40383

(859) 879-1812

www.woodfordreserve.com

Don't Miss:

The Bourbon

Woodford is L&G's (Labrot & Graham's) premium bourbon. I love to serve it to guests and on special occasions. But for cooking and flavored cocktails, I use Old Forrester. The venerable bourbon, also by L&G, costs half as much but stands among the best whiskeys.

Amid the rolling hills of the bluegrass and tucked among lush horse farms stands one of the most beautiful distilleries in the world. A holy sanctuary for bourbon lovers everywhere, Woodford Reserve beckons those who want to spend an afternoon among the finer things life has to offer. Guests may taste whiskey throughout the year, but during the summers the distillery opens a porch for casual dining overlooking the facility. Visitors will find some of the best kitchen creations ever to contain the South's favorite drink.

Steak Salad

Steak

- ½ cup olive oil
- 2 Tbsp. ketchup
- 1 Tbsp. bourbon
- 1 Tbsp. soy sauce
- 1 tsp. pepper
- ½ tsp. salt
- 2 lb. top sirloin steak

Vegetables

- 12 small round red potatoes
- 1 tsp. salt
- 1 cup broccoli florets
- 1 cup cherry tomatoes, halved
- ⅔ cup thin red bell pepper strips
- ⅔ cup finely chopped green onions
- 4 medium carrots, cut thinly into diagonal slices
- 2 small zucchini, cut into thin strips

Basil Vinaigrette

- ½ cup olive oil
- 2 Tbsp. finely chopped fresh basil
- 2 Tbsp. finely chopped fresh flat leaf parsley
- 2 Tbsp. balsamic vinegar
- 1 Tbsp. capers
- 1 tsp. Dijon mustard
- ½ tsp. salt
- ½ tsp. pepper
- Dash of sugar

* Diner Secret: Cook the steak to medium-rare to keep it tender and juicy.

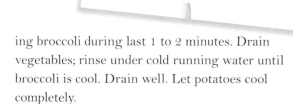

1. **Prepare Steak:** Stir together first 6 ingredients in an 11- x 7-inch baking dish. Add steak to marinade, turning to coat. Cover and marinate in the refrigerator 45 minutes, turning occasionally.

2. **Meanwhile, prepare Vegetables:** Bring 2 qt. water, potatoes, and 1 tsp. salt to a boil in a medium saucepan; reduce heat, and simmer, uncovered, 18 to 20 minutes or until tender, adding broccoli during last 1 to 2 minutes. Drain vegetables; rinse under cold running water until broccoli is cool. Drain well. Let potatoes cool completely.

3. **Meanwhile, prepare Basil Vinaigrette:** Whisk together all ingredients in a small bowl. Cover and chill until ready to use.

4. Place potatoes, broccoli, tomatoes, and next 4 ingredients in a large bowl. Cover and chill until ready to use.

5. Coat cold cooking grate of grill with cooking spray, and place on grill. Preheat grill to 350° to 400° (medium-high) heat. Remove steak from marinade, discarding marinade. Place steak on cooking grate, and grill 6 minutes on each side or until a thermometer registers 145° (medium-rare). Transfer steak to a plate; let cool completely. Cut steak into bite-size strips.

6. Add steak to vegetables. Drizzle with Basil Vinaigrette; toss well. **Makes 5 to 6 servings.**

✳ Diner Secret: Patting steaks dry ensures the good browning necessary to develop rich flavor.

Rib-Eye Steaks

| | cup bourbon
2 tsp. minced fresh sage
2 garlic cloves, minced
2 (12-oz.) boneless rib-eye steaks
| tsp. kosher salt
¼ tsp. freshly ground pepper
2 Tbsp. olive oil
Spiced Butter

1. Stir together bourbon, sage, and garlic in an 11- x 7-inch baking dish; add steaks, turning to coat. Cover and marinate at room temperature for up to 1 hour, turning once.
2. Remove steaks from marinade, discarding marinade. Pat steaks dry with paper towels; sprinkle with salt and pepper.
3. Heat a large cast-iron skillet over medium-high heat 5 minutes. Add oil to pan; add steaks, and cook 4 minutes. Turn steaks over, and cook 2 more minutes. Transfer steaks to 2 individual serving plates. Top each steak with a dollop of Spiced Butter. **Makes 2 servings.**

Spiced Butter

¼ cup unsalted butter, softened
2 tsp. paprika
| tsp. dry mustard
| tsp. ground coriander
| tsp. ground celery seeds
| tsp. ground chipotle chile pepper
½ tsp. salt
¼ tsp. pepper

1. Place all ingredients in a small bowl. Beat at medium speed with an electric mixer until smooth. **Makes 6 tablespoons.**

Louisiana

Best Drive

The River Road

ew spots capture the beauty of the antebellum South better than the splendorous homes of the Mississippi River Road. Mark Twain noted this drive: "From Baton Rouge to New Orleans, the great sugar plantations border both sides of the river all the way…a most home-like and happy-looking region." Oak Alley may be the most famous example of grand homes, but you'll also want to visit Houmas House, Ormond, Bocage, Evergreen, and San Francisco. Today the drive is a mishmash of prewar beauty and strip-mall eyesores, but no Southern sojourn is complete without a drive here. **Length:** 70 miles

LOLA

Covington, Louisiana

GPS COORDINATES:

Lat./Long. 30.477941,-90.096215

517 N. New Hampshire Street 70433
(985) 892-4992

www.lolacovington.com

Don't Miss:

Railroad Depot

Part of LOLA's charm is its setting—the old railroad depot in Covington. Brick walls, vintage light fixtures, and a romantic travel feel make a visit here seem like the beginning of an adventure. Be sure to check out the kitchen, which is lodged in an adjoining caboose.

Louisiana brims with delicious bread puddings, a signature dish of the region. For one of the best, try LOLA's recipe at right. To me, a great bread pudding must be dense, not so sweet as to knock you over, and contain some crust and crunch (otherwise, it's just a bowl of goo). LOLA's Nealy Frentz makes it just right, using her signature bread and her cooking skills honed from years of restaurant life in New Orleans.

White Chocolate Bread Pudding

6   large eggs
⅔   cup sugar
1   tsp. vanilla extract
½   tsp. ground cinnamon
2½   cups heavy cream
¼   cup bourbon or whiskey
1   (12-oz.) loaf French bread, cut into
     1-inch cubes
1   (4-oz.) white chocolate baking bar, chopped
6   Tbsp. cold butter, cut into pieces
White Chocolate Sauce

1. Preheat oven to 400°. Whisk eggs in a large bowl; whisk in sugar, vanilla, and cinnamon. Stir in cream and bourbon. Add bread cubes, white chocolate, and butter, stirring well. Pour bread mixture into a lightly greased 13- x 9-inch baking dish.

2. Bake, uncovered, at 400° for 35 minutes or until set and golden. Serve warm with White Chocolate Sauce. **Makes 8 to 10 servings.**

White Chocolate Sauce

2   cups heavy cream
2   (4-oz.) white chocolate baking bars, chopped
¼   cup bourbon or whiskey

1. Place cream in a 2-qt. heavy saucepan. Bring to a simmer over medium heat, stirring often. Remove from heat; add chopped white chocolate and bourbon, whisking until smooth. **Makes 2⅔ cups.**

* Diner Secret: Oysters are available in different sizes, standard or select. If large, chop them for this stew.

Oyster Stew with Brie and Spinach

2   (16-oz.) containers standard oysters, undrained
½   cup plus 2 Tbsp. butter
½   large onion, diced
3   celery ribs, diced
2   garlic cloves, minced
½   cup all-purpose flour
2   cups milk
1   Tbsp. pepper
2   tsp. salt
1½ tsp. Worcestershire sauce
½   tsp. dried thyme
⅛   tsp. hot sauce
1   bay leaf
1½ (6-oz.) packages fresh baby spinach
1   (4-oz.) Brie round, diced
¼   cup chopped fresh parsley

1. Combine oysters with oyster liquid and 1 qt. cold water in a Dutch oven. Bring oysters to a simmer over high heat just until edges begin to curl (about 8 minutes). Remove from heat; strain, reserving 6 cups oyster stock. Set oysters aside.
2. Meanwhile, melt butter in Dutch oven over medium-high heat. Add onion and celery; sauté 6 minutes or until vegetables are tender. Add garlic; sauté 2 minutes. Stir in flour; cook, stirring constantly, 1 minute. Gradually stir in milk and reserved oyster stock. Stir in pepper and next 5 ingredients. Bring just to a boil; reduce heat, and simmer, uncovered, 20 minutes.
3. Stir in spinach; cook 1 to 2 minutes or until wilted. Add Brie, stirring until cheese melts. Remove and discard bay leaf. Stir in parsley and oysters just before serving. **Makes 10 cups.**

From tail to hoof, this is the "best stop" for hog lovers.

The Best Stop Supermarket

Scott, Louisiana

I believe boudin should be eaten in the parking lot of the store where you bought it. Best Stop, as its name implies, ranks as a stellar place to eat some of the best boudin in the state. It's made here, of course, along with cracklins, boudin balls, and beef jerky. At any time of day you'll find patrons lined up to order up Best Stop's delicious sausage. The store isn't fancy, but owner Dana Cormier insists upon the finest cuts of meat, which make all the difference.

Best Stop's spicy seasoning, which contains no MSG (a rarity in the world of store-bought spices), can be ordered through the mail. Oh, and if you just can't live without a boudin ball, Best Stop will ship you some on dried ice. Hallelujah. Visit www.beststopinscott.com or call (337) 233-5805 to order.

Food Find:

Richard's Seafood Patio

Abbeville, Louisiana

GPS COORDINATES:
Lat./Long. 29.968174,-92.166006

5165 South Henry Street 70510
(337) 893-1146

Don't Miss:

Boiled Platters

Second-generation owners Calvin and Roxanne Richard are a creative duo. Not only are their recipes inventive, but even their boiled platters are patented for the unique way Calvin designed an expandable area for discarded shrimp, crab, and crawfish shells. No wonder they're still going strong.

Deep in bayou country, you'll find a tin shed on the side of a lonely road. Inside, Louisiana's three seasons are celebrated with abandon. I'm talking about crawfish season, crab season, and shrimp season. For more than 50 years, those in the know have come to Richard's. So while there's no longer a patio, the restaurant still boils its seafood in the traditional way (by putting the spices in the water), which means when you bite into the sweet, succulent crabmeat, it packs all the spicy punch of a Louisiana evening.

Drunk Shrimp

If you choose to use shrimp with the heads on, use 1½ pounds.

2   (12-oz.) bottles beer
2   tsp. salt
2   tsp. dried crushed red pepper
1   lb. unpeeled, large raw shrimp (31/40 count)

1. Bring first 3 ingredients to a boil in a large saucepan; add shrimp, and return to a boil. Cook 2 minutes; remove from heat, and strain. **Makes 3 to 4 appetizer servings.**

* Diner Secret: Use your favorite brand of beer to sauce these shrimp—just don't use light beer.

Corn-and-Crab Chowder

Loads of fresh crabmeat dress up this convenience-style soup.

2   (10¾-oz.) cans cream of potato soup
1   (10¾-oz.) can cream of mushroom soup
1   (8-oz.) package cream cheese, softened
3   cups half-and-half
1   lb. fresh crabmeat
1   (15.25-oz.) can sweet whole kernel corn, drained
1   (14¾-oz.) can cream-style corn
1   tsp. Old Bay seasoning

1. Process first 3 ingredients in a blender until smooth, stopping to scrape down sides as needed. Transfer cream cheese mixture to a Dutch oven. Stir in half-and-half and remaining ingredients.
2. Cover and bring to a boil; reduce heat to medium, and cook 10 minutes, stirring often. **Makes 12 cups.**

* Diner Secret: Old Bay seasoning gives salt and spice in one dose.

Café Beignet

New Orleans, Louisiana

GPS COORDINATES:
Lat./Long. 29.95534,-90.067106

334-B Royal Street 70130
(504) 524-5530
www.cafebeignet.com

Don't Miss:

Great Antiques

Café Beignet is owned by Peter Moss, who also owns Keil's Antiques across the street. Keil's is the oldest antiques store in New Orleans, and, in my opinion, the most fabulous. It's loaded with treasures ranging from simple walking sticks to elaborate chandeliers. After you've had a little breakfast (or brunch), spend some time exploring.

After a long night on Bourbon Street, many visitors to the Big Easy find it a little hard to get up in the morning. Leave it to the Crescent City to invent the perfect hangover cure: strong chicory coffee and sugary, decadent beignets. If you've never had the two, you're missing out. A café au lait at Café Beignet may be savored in the restaurant's gorgeous garden or beneath its rustic, curved ceiling. The atmosphere is quiet, relaxed, and as non-touristy as you'll find in the French Quarter. Plus the beignets are the best in the city.

Beignets

Take charge of this sticky dough by dusting your hands and work surface with flour before rolling out the dough.

2   cups self-rising flour
3   Tbsp. chilled shortening, cut into pieces
¾   cup hot water
1   Tbsp. sugar
1   tsp. vanilla extract (optional)
Vegetable oil
Wax paper
Powdered sugar

1. Place flour in a large bowl. Cut shortening into flour with a pastry blender or fork until crumbly. Combine hot water and sugar in a small bowl, stirring until sugar dissolves. Let cool to room temperature; add vanilla, if desired. Add sugar mixture to flour mixture, stirring with a fork just until dry ingredients are moistened. (Dough will be sticky.)

2. Pour oil to depth of 3 inches in a Dutch oven; heat to 375°.

3. Meanwhile, turn dough out onto a well floured surface, and knead lightly 3 or 4 times. Roll dough to ¼-inch thickness; cut into 2-inch squares, and place on wax paper-lined baking sheets. Let dough rest 10 minutes.

4. Fry beignets, in batches, 1 minute on each side or until golden brown. Drain on paper towels, and dust generously with powdered sugar. Serve hot. **Makes 1 dozen.**

Louisiana

107

Pat's Fisherman's Wharf

Henderson, Louisiana

GPS COORDINATES:

Lat./Long. 30.314652,-91.788608

1008 Henderson Levee Road 70517

(337) 228-7512

www. patsfishermanswharf.com

Don't Miss:

Étouffée

What's the difference between camp-style étouffée and the more traditional version? Butter. Camp-style étouffée starts with oil, and thus was easier to make outside of a fully-stocked kitchen. In the recipe at right a half stick of butter can replace the oil.

Shake the hand of Pat Huval, now well into his eighties, and he'll cheerily tell you, "I'm the man that mudbugs made." What started as a simple gas station selling the crawfish most people considered only good for bait has grown into a restaurant, roux plant, seafood-processing center, dance hall, and hotel. It's all on the banks of the Atchafalaya River. Though the business has grown, regulars still love to come in and have the classic camp-style crawfish or shrimp étouffée and a cold beer. Ahh, swamp heaven.

Shrimp and Crab Étouffée

Buy the freshest crab available for this rich seafood entrée.

- 1   lb. unpeeled, large raw shrimp (31/40 count)
- 2   Tbsp. canola oil
- 2   medium onions, chopped
- 2   green bell peppers, chopped
- 1   tsp. salt
- 1   tsp. paprika
- ¼   tsp. ground red pepper
- 1   lb. fresh jumbo lump crabmeat, drained

Hot cooked rice

1. Peel shrimp; devein, if desired. Heat oil in a large skillet over medium-high heat. Add onions and green pepper; sauté 10 minutes or until vegetables are tender.

2. Add shrimp, ½ cup water, salt, paprika, and red pepper. Cook 3 minutes or until shrimp turn pink. Stir in crabmeat. Cook over medium heat 1 to 2 minutes or just until thoroughly heated. Serve over rice. **Makes 4 servings.**

Enjoy music and the river view at the club behind the restaurant.

✱ Diner Secret: A squeeze of lemon gives a bright finish to these seafood rolls stuffed with crab.

Snapper Patrick

1   lb. fresh lump crabmeat, drained
4   (9-oz.) red snapper fillets, skinned
1   tsp. salt
1   tsp. garlic powder
1   tsp. ground red pepper
¼   cup butter, melted
Lemon wedges

1. Preheat oven to 400°. Pick crabmeat, removing any bits of shell. Cut snapper fillets in half lengthwise. Top each fillet with about ⅓ cup crabmeat; roll up fillets, and secure with wooden picks.
2. Stir together salt, garlic powder, and red pepper. Combine butter and 2 Tbsp. water in a 13- x 9-inch pan. Sprinkle 1 tsp. seasoning mixture over butter mixture. Arrange rollups in butter mixture. Sprinkle rollups with remaining 2 tsp. seasoning mixture.
3. Bake, uncovered, at 400° for 16 to 18 minutes or until fish flakes when tested with a fork. Spoon pan drippings over rollups before serving, if desired. Serve with lemon wedges.
Makes 8 servings.

Rubbernecker Wonder:
New Orleans, Louisiana
Voodoo Temple

I'm not a superstitious person, nor do I believe in voodoo. (Though you'll find an ample number of folks in these parts who do… or don't dare not to.) I decided to give black magic a try because sometimes the road brings out the worst in a car, and round about the Big Easy I began to think my Cadillac was cursed. So I took it to the High Priestess Miriam and her Voodoo Temple to get the demons out of the engine bay. She burned all kinds of nasty-smelling stuff, murmured a few incantations, and charged me a modest fee. Did it help? Well, I made it home. She might be able to fix your vintage Caddy too.

Stay on the good side of that sweet face or your ride home may backfire.

Look!

R&M's Boiling Point

New Iberia, Louisiana

GPS COORDINATES:
Lat./Long. 29.928806,-91.742106

7413 Highway 90 West 70560
(337) 365-7596.

Don't Miss:

Stuffed Jalapeños

The over-the-top, hot jalapeño is stuffed
with shrimp and deep fried. Ain't it good to
be in Louisiana?

N ext to a small cement plant, this tiny
spot serves up some huge flavors of the
Cajun country. Sinks in the middle of the
dining room will be your first clue that your lunch
will be messy. But oh, few messes taste this good!
I suggest you begin with the fried alligator. Cut
into chicken-finger-size strips fried to a deep brown
and served with an excellent tartar sauce and fresh
lemon. Then move on to a half order of shrimp and
crawfish. The shrimp are as big as you'll ever find
and spiced just right. The platter of crawfish could
double as the hub of a Mack Truck—the mound of
deep scarlet crustaceans will burn your lips and
leave your eyes watering (and I mean that in the
best of ways).

Crab Au Gratin

This dish is best made with fresh-picked crabmeat straight from the Gulf.

- ½ cup butter
- 3 cups chopped onions (2 medium)
- ¼ cup chopped celery
- 2 lb. fresh jumbo lump crabmeat, drained
- ⅓ cup all-purpose flour
- 1 (12-oz.) can evaporated milk
- 1 tsp. salt
- ¼ tsp. hot sauce
- ⅛ tsp. ground red pepper
- 2 oz. freshly grated Parmigiano-Reggiano cheese

1. Preheat oven to 350°. Melt butter in a 4-qt. saucepan or Dutch oven over medium-high heat. Add chopped onions and celery; cook, stirring often, 8 minutes or until softened.

2. Meanwhile, pick crabmeat, removing any bits of shell. Remove onion mixture from heat; sprinkle with flour, stirring constantly. Gradually stir in milk. Cook, stirring constantly, over medium heat 2 minutes or until thickened. Stir in salt, hot sauce, and pepper. Add crabmeat.

3. Pour crab mixture into a lightly greased 13- x 9-inch baking dish; sprinkle with cheese.

4. Bake, uncovered, at 350° for 30 minutes or until golden and bubbly. **Makes 12 servings.**

Greetings From MARYLAND

State Capitol in

State Flower
Black-eyed Susan

From ruffled feathers...

...to feathered caps and ruffled collars,
Maryland promises uncommon sights.

Maryland

Best Drive

The Chesapeake Country Scenic Byway

From colonial towns to quaint fishing villages, this drive will take you through some of the most gorgeous scenery on the Chesapeake. The names you'll see along the way (Kingstown, Georgetown, Queen Anne's County) evoke our country's British roots. Go to the beach for some water sports or head out charter fishing at one of the many towns along the Eastern Shore. Love waterfowl? Enjoy the bay's amazing birds by exploring the Eastern Neck National Wildlife Refuge. Make sure to take your binoculars. **Length:** 80 miles

Maryland

115

Bel-Loc Diner

Baltimore, Maryland

GPS COORDINATES:

Lat./Long. 39.397342,-76.563237

1700 East Joppa Road 21234

(410) 668-2525

Don't Miss:

Rice Pudding

The creamy rice pudding, featured at right, is a masterpiece in a little bowl. Nowadays it's popular to eat with a dollop of whipped cream, but for the classic experience, dump two coffee creamers over your pudding. That's the way the old timers roll.

Walking into the Bel-Loc takes the hungry patron straight back to 1964. The stainless steel, formica, and tile give the place a classic diner appearance, along with the snappy waitresses in perfectly pressed uniforms. The coffee is always hot, the fare is simple but delicious, and you can't ask for a more relaxing spot to take a break from the road. And speaking of, the road is where this diner got its name. The restaurant sits at the intersection of the Beltway and Loch Raven Road.

Bel-Loc Rice Pudding

This is a very sweet rice pudding—simple, yet comfortingly creamy.

2⅔ cups milk
⅔ cup medium-grain rice
¼ tsp. salt
1½ tsp. vanilla extract
3 egg yolks
1 cup sugar
½ cup milk
Garnish: Ground cinnamon

1. Combine milk and next 3 ingredients in a medium saucepan. Cover and cook over low heat about 40 minutes or until rice is tender, stirring occasionally.

2. Whisk together eggs yolks, sugar, and ½ cup milk in a medium bowl. Gradually stir about one-fourth of hot rice mixture into eggs; add egg mixture to remaining hot rice mixture, stirring constantly. Cook over low heat, stirring constantly, until mixture reaches 160° and is thickened and bubbly (about 10 minutes). Garnish with cinnamon, if desired. Serve either warm or chilled. **Makes 4 to 6 servings.**

Carpenter Street Saloon

St. Michael's, Maryland

GPS COORDINATES:

Lat./Long. 38.786165,-76.224279

113 S Talbot Street 21663

(410) 745-5111

Don't Miss:

Tipsy Chicken

More akin to a classic chicken marsala, albeit with a bit more garlic, this dish pairs perfectly with Carpenter Street Saloon's trademark Bloody Marys. Instead of using ordinary pre-made mixes, Carpenter makes their own drink mix, which is a closely guarded secret.

A beer, laughter, and good friends make the common bar a true pub. And that's the kind of atmosphere you'll find at the Carpenter Street Saloon. The humor starts with owner Diana Mautz. "I bought it after I had too much to drink one St. Patrick's Day, figuring it would be a good way to get through a midlife crisis for a couple of years." Forty years later, she's still serving regulars, laughing with guests, and dishing out culinary surprises you might not expect to find in a simple bar.

Tipsy Chicken

Marsala simmers rich goodness into sautéed chicken breasts for this upscale entrée.

- 2 (6-oz.) skinned and boned chicken breasts
- ¼ tsp. salt
- ¼ tsp. pepper
- ¼ cup all-purpose flour
- 2 Tbsp. olive oil
- 1 cup sliced fresh mushrooms
- 1 Tbsp. minced garlic
- ⅔ cup Marsala
- 2 Tbsp. butter
- 2 Tbsp. chopped fresh flat-leaf parsley

1. Place chicken between 2 sheets of plastic wrap, and flatten to ½-inch thickness using a rolling pin or flat side of a meat mallet. Sprinkle chicken with salt and pepper; dredge in flour, shaking off excess.

2. Cook chicken in hot oil in a large skillet over medium-high heat 2 to 3 minutes on each side or until browned. Remove from skillet, and keep warm.

3. Sauté mushrooms and garlic in drippings 3 minutes or until tender. Return chicken to pan. Add Marsala, and simmer 3 minutes, stirring to loosen particles from bottom of skillet. Add butter, stirring until melted. Remove from heat, and sprinkle with parsley. **Makes 2 servings.**

Boordy Vineyards

Hydes, Maryland

Established in 1945 by the R.B. Deford family, this 240-acre vineyard in the Baltimore countryside is Maryland's oldest family-run winery. Sip their Chardonnay Maryland Barrel Select or Eisling.

Open 10 a.m.-5 p.m. Monday-Saturday and 1-5 p.m. Sunday. Tours for 10 or more at 2 p.m. and 3:30 p.m. daily. For more information visit www.boordy.com.

Food Find:

Chick & Ruth's Delly

Annapolis, Maryland

GPS COORDINATES:
Lat./Long. 38.977724,-76.489861

165 Main Street 21401
(410) 269-6737
www.chickandruths.com

Don't Miss:

The Governor's Booth

Being just steps from the statehouse, Chick & Ruth's has a booth reserved for the governor. It's roped off so that he can dash in at a moment's notice, swill a 6-pound shake (yep, it's on the menu), and get back to business.

✱ Diner Secret: The key to the crisp is to press hash flat and let it cook undisturbed.

A favorite of sailors and friends of sailors everywhere, Chick & Ruth's Delly should be the first place you moor your boat for breakfast. Located on the main drag, the restaurant can't be missed with its green awning and bright-orange paintwork. The decor isn't subtle, and neither are menu options such as a corned beef hash and unbeatable crab omelette. Mornings are a glimpse of America at its best: Go at 8 a.m. and prepare to say the "Pledge of Allegiance." Linger around, and second-generation owner Ted Leditt may perform some of his amazing magic tricks for you.

Corned Beef Hash

- 1½ lb. potatoes, peeled and finely diced
- 1 lb. corned beef, cut into ¼-inch slices and coarsely chopped
- 1 medium onion, quartered
- ¼ tsp. salt
- ½ tsp. pepper
- 3 Tbsp. vegetable oil

1. Cook potatoes in a large saucepan of boiling water to cover 3 minutes or until tender; drain. Place potatoes in a large bowl. Pulse corned beef in a food processor 6 to 8 times or until very finely chopped; add to potatoes in bowl.
2. Pulse onion 2 to 3 times or until finely chopped; add to potato mixture. Sprinkle with salt and pepper; stir well.
3. Heat oil in a large skillet over medium-high heat. Add corned beef mixture; press flat with a spatula. Cook 8 minutes; turn and cook 9 minutes or until crisp and well browned, turning and pressing flat with spatula every 3 minutes. **Makes 6 to 8 servings.**

Rubbernecker Wonder:
Anapolis, Maryland
Best Place to Salute

As an officer in the United States Navy, I have a natural soft spot for the capital of Maryland. The town's walkable streets, quaint shops, and rich nautical history make Annapolis the perfect place to spend a weekend. Named for Anne, the Queen of England, this beautiful city is convenient to Baltimore-Washington Airport.

Make sure to swing by the Naval Academy. The fantastic gift shop and stunning chapel will convert you to a fan of the Blue and Gold. I always pick up a few "BEAT ARMY" pins for good luck during the next Army-Navy game.

Annapolis is often called "The Sailing Capital of the World." You'll find plenty of opportunities to get out on the bay and enjoy one of the most navigable bodies of water in the world.

Take a leisurely stroll along the dock of this maritime port.

Look!

Faidley's Seafood

Baltimore, Maryland

GPS COORDINATES:
Lat./Long. 39.291453,-76.622408

203 North Paca 21201
(410) 727-4898
www.faidleyscrabcakes.com

Don't Miss:

Oysters by the Dozen

Much of Faidley's oyster supply comes straight from the nearby James River, and they're among the best I've tried. As the signs say above the bar, "Forget Viagra. Eat Oysters. (No prescription required)."

An oldie but a goody: Faidley's five generations of family caretakers have made the seafood-supply house a legend in these parts. The place is truly a market, where you can buy the freshest fish, oysters, crab, and so forth. But it's also home to the most unbelievably delicious crab cake in town—just the right mix of sweet jumbo lump crab and filler. Words can't describe that kind of perfection, which is made all the better by eating it while standing next to a long wooden table with a bunch of strangers sharing in the delight.

Faidley's Crab Cake

If desired, pan-fry cakes in about 3 Tbsp. butter instead of oil until golden.

½   cup mayonnaise
1   Tbsp. Dijon mustard
1   Tbsp. Worcestershire sauce
½   tsp. hot sauce
1   egg
1   lb. fresh jumbo lump crabmeat, drained
1   cup coarsely crushed saltine crackers
1   qt. vegetable oil

1. Whisk together first 5 ingredients until blended. Stir in crabmeat and crackers. Shape mixture into 8 patties. Place patties on a wax paper–lined baking sheet; cover and chill 1 hour.

2. Heat oil to 375° in a large deep skillet. Fry patties, in batches, in hot oil 3 minutes on each side or until golden. Drain on a wire rack over paper towels. **Makes 8 servings.**

Faidley's Seafood has been a family affair since 1886.

✳ Diner Secret: A generous mix of crisp chopped vegetables adds fresh flavor.

Macaroni Salad

Reduce the sugar in this sweetened salad to ¼ cup if you'd like.

1   cup mayonnaise
⅓   cup sugar
1   Tbsp. dried basil
¾   tsp. salt
½   tsp. pepper
3   cups elbow macaroni, cooked
1   cup chopped seeded cucumber
½   cup chopped carrot
½   cup sliced radishes
½   cup finely chopped green onions

1. Stir together first 5 ingredients in a large bowl. Add hot macaroni and remaining ingredients, stirring to coat. Cover and chill at least 2 hours. **Makes 8 to 10 servings.**

Obrycki's

Baltimore, Maryland

GPS COORDINATES:

Lat./Long. 39.28917,-76.592744

1727 East Pratt Street 21231

(410) 732-6399

www.obryckis.com

Don't Miss:

The Accoutrements

The oldest crab house in town rolls out butcher paper, bibs, and mallets when you order your crabs steamed and spiced. The place is a cacophony of hammering, beating, and bludgeoning—making this a singular seafood experience you won't forget.

You're going to be perplexed when you pull up to this Baltimore legend. Nothing about the plain awning or building hints to the crab wonderland that waits inside. But Obrycki's is the spot in town to have crab of all kinds: crab soup, crab balls, crab cakes, crab imperial, crab cocktail, soft shell crab, and my favorites—crab bisque and crab dip. As if those delights weren't enough, they offer a crab meat omelet so rich you might have to head back to bed afterward.

Crab Dip

1   (8-oz.) package cream cheese, softened
¾   cup (3 oz.) shredded Cheddar cheese, divided
3   Tbsp. sour cream
1   Tbsp. mayonnaise
⅓   cup fresh breadcrumbs
1   Tbsp. minced onion
1   Tbsp. hot sauce
½   tsp. Worcestershire sauce
½   tsp. Old Bay seasoning
Dash of salt
Dash of pepper
1   lb. fresh lump crabmeat, drained

1. Preheat oven to 350°. Combine cream cheese, ¼ cup Cheddar, sour cream, and mayonnaise in a mixing bowl. Beat at medium speed with an electric mixer until smooth. Stir in breadcrumbs and next 6 ingredients. Fold in crabmeat.

2. Spoon mixture into a lightly greased 8-inch square baking dish. Sprinkle with remaining ½ cup Cheddar cheese.

3. Bake, uncovered, at 350° for 30 minutes or until bubbly and golden. **Makes 8 to 10 servings.**

Crab Meat Omelet

2   Tbsp. butter, divided
¼   cup diced onion
¼   cup diced green bell pepper
3   large eggs
¼   tsp. Old Bay seasoning
¼   cup (1 oz.) shredded Cheddar cheese
¼   cup diced tomato
4   oz. fresh lump crabmeat, drained
Old Bay seasoning (optional)

1. Melt 1 Tbsp. butter in a 12-inch nonstick skillet over medium heat. Add onion and bell pepper; sauté 3 minutes or until tender. Remove vegetables from skillet; set aside.

2. Whisk together eggs and ¼ tsp. Old Bay seasoning. Melt remaining 1 Tbsp. butter in skillet over medium-high heat. Pour egg mixture into skillet. As egg starts to cook, gently lift edges of omelet with a spatula, and tilt pan so uncooked portion flows underneath. Sprinkle 1 side of omelet with cheese, sautéed vegetables, tomato, and crabmeat. Fold in half. Cook over medium-low heat 1 minute or until cheese melts. Slide cooked omelet onto a serving plate, and season with additional Old Bay seasoning, if desired. Serve with buttered toast. **Makes 1 serving.**

✱ Diner Secret: A bit of Old Bay lends a distinctive savory accent to this colorful seafood omelet.

Greetings from MISSISSIPPI

State Capital in Jackson

State Flower

Stop and smell the coffee. Everything in the Magnolia State ambles at a slower pace.

COFFEE · ESPRESSO

Mississippi

Best Drive

The Natchez Trace

Winding from the gorgeous town of Natchez to country music's home in Nashville, the Trace can boast roots dating back hundreds of years. For much of our nation's history, it was the easiest way to the port cities along the Mississippi River. The route was full of early American culture: bandits, cowboys, Indians, preachers, traders, and the like. Take it today, and you'll be following in the footsteps of some of our most famous forefathers, from Andrew Jackson to Meriwether Lewis. Today, its slow speed limits, perfect pavement, and many iconic Mississippi stops in the Delta make it a splendid way to spend a few days on the road. **Length:** 444 miles

Ajax Diner

Oxford, Mississippi

GPS COORDINATES:

Lat./Long. 34.366753,-89.519078

118 Courthouse Square 38655

(662) 232-8880

www.ajaxdiner.net

Don't Miss:

"The Deuce"

"The Deuce" is a giant, juicy, ¾-pound hamburger made with Black Angus beef. Roll up your sleeves and wear a bib—this burger will leave you covered after two or three bites.

I've never been to Ajax when it wasn't totally slammed. Why? Because the cool college hangout dishes out some of Oxford's best fare—at any price point. If you go on Friday, you'll be treated to a special called "Chicken Enchilada Casserole." Try it. Spicy, juicy chicken and fabulous peppers are wrapped up in tender flour tortillas. Plus, you get your choice of two vegetables and a huge square of jalapeño cornbread.

Corn-and-Tomato Salad

½   cup chopped fresh flat-leaf parsley
½   cup sour cream
½   cup mayonnaise
⅓   cup apple cider vinegar
1½   tsp. kosher salt
1½   tsp. dried oregano
1   tsp. pepper
1¾   cups grape tomatoes, halved
3   (12-oz.) packages frozen white shoepeg
     corn, thawed
1   green bell pepper, diced (1 cup)
½   red onion, diced (1 cup)

1. Stir together first 7 ingredients in a large bowl. Add tomatoes and remaining ingredients, stirring well. Serve with a slotted spoon. **Makes 10 to 12 servings.**

Sweet Potato Casserole

4   large sweet potatoes (about 3¼ lb.)
2   cups firmly packed brown sugar, divided
1¼   cups butter, melted and divided
½   cup milk
1   tsp. vanilla extract
4   large eggs, beaten
¼   cup all-purpose flour
1   cup pecan pieces
3   cups miniature marshmallows

1. Preheat oven to 400°. Bake sweet potatoes at 400° for 1 hour or until tender. Let stand until cool to touch (about 20 minutes); peel and mash sweet potatoes. Reduce oven temperature to 375°.
2. Beat mashed sweet potatoes, 1¼ cups brown sugar, 1 cup butter, and next 3 ingredients at medium speed with an electric mixer until smooth. Spoon potato mixture into a greased 13- x 9-inch baking dish.
3. Combine flour and remaining ½ cup brown sugar in a medium bowl; add remaining ¼ cup butter, stirring until crumbly. Stir in pecans. Sprinkle topping over potatoes. Cover and bake at 375° for 1 hour. Uncover and sprinkle marshmallows over topping. Bake 10 more minutes or until marshmallows are golden. Let stand 10 minutes before serving. **Makes 10 to 12 servings.**

Squash Casserole

1½   yellow onions, halved vertically
½   cup butter
4   lb. yellow squash, sliced
1   tsp. kosher salt
1   tsp. freshly ground pepper
1½   cups Japanese breadcrumbs (panko)
1   cup freshly grated Parmesan cheese

1. Preheat oven to 375°. Cut onion halves crosswise into thin slices. Melt butter in a large deep skillet over medium-high heat. Add onions; sauté 5 minutes or until tender. Add squash, salt, and pepper. Bring to a boil; cover, reduce heat to medium, and simmer 25 minutes or until squash is tender, stirring occasionally.
2. Uncover, and cook 5 more minutes. Remove from heat. Add breadcrumbs; toss lightly. Spoon squash mixture into a lightly greased 13- x 9-inch baking dish. Sprinkle with cheese.
3. Bake, uncovered, at 375° for 30 minutes or until casserole is bubbly. **Makes 10 to 12 servings.**

Doe's Eat Place

Greenville, Mississippi

GPS COORDINATES:

Lat./Long. 33.415688,-91.056127

502 Nelson Street 38701

(662) 334-3315

www.doeseatplace.com

Don't Miss:

The Bit Bowl

Aunt Florence, the salad queen, has been making Doe's secret salad for 64 years. I flirted shamelessly with her to get this recipe. Remember her two tips: Use fresh lemon juice and fresh minced garlic. And make sure your lettuce, tomato, and onion are "cold, cold, cold."

The slap of the screen door brings you into the kitchen of this old Greenville institution. That's right, you walk right into the kitchen. Just say "Hey y'all" and keep on moving towards the back if you want to look like a regular. Doe's, which has been in business since 1941, puts on no airs. Second-generation owners, brothers Charles and Doe Signa, will happily tell you that their joint is a little battered and on the wrong side of town. No matter—the steaks are the best in Mississippi, and the broiled shrimp has a spicy tartness you won't soon forget.

Broiled Shrimp

- 24 unpeeled, large raw shrimp
- ¼ cup roasted garlic butter, melted
- 2 Tbsp. fresh lemon juice
- ¾ tsp. Worcestershire sauce
- ½ tsp. Creole seasoning
- ½ tsp. paprika
- ½ tsp. dried Italian seasoning
- Hot cooked rice (optional)

1. Preheat broiler with oven rack 3 inches from heat. Peel shrimp, leaving tails on; devein, if desired. Place shrimp in a lightly greased broiler pan. Combine melted garlic butter, lemon juice, and next 4 ingredients, stirring well. Drizzle garlic butter mixture over shrimp. Broil 4 to 5 minutes or just until shrimp turn pink. Serve over rice, if desired. **Makes 2 servings.**
Note: We tested with Land O Lakes Roasted Garlic Butter Spread in a tub.

Aunt Florence's Bit Bowl

- ⅓ cup olive oil
- ¼ cup fresh lemon juice
- ½ tsp. salt
- 1 garlic clove, pressed
- 1 small head iceberg lettuce, torn (5 cups)
- 1 large tomato, chopped
- 1 small red onion, thinly sliced

1. Whisk together olive oil and next 3 ingredients in a small bowl. Combine lettuce, tomato, and onion in a large bowl; gradually add enough olive oil mixture to coat leaves, tossing gently. Serve salad with remaining olive oil mixture, if desired. **Makes 4 servings.**

Chill your bulk ingredients before preparing this tossed salad so it's ready to serve.

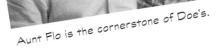

Aunt Flo is the cornerstone of Doe's.

The Castle at Dunleith Plantation

Natchez, Mississippi

GPS COORDINATES:
Lat./Long. 31.560444,-91.403171

84 Homochitto Street 39120

(601) 446-8500

www.dunleith.com

Don't Miss: The Castlette

Chef Brad Seyfarth's "Castlette" is a splurge in every sense. Fresh shrimp, scallops, and crab are baked in a creamy garlic and Parmesan sauce to decadent perfection. "It's easy to make at home," says Brad, "and don't worry if you can't find truffles. It also works well without them."

Behind the graceful columns and Spanish moss-draped live oaks of this antebellum mansion, guests will find Natchez's most elegant restaurant. The fact that the Castle is in a former horse stable at an old plantation might lead one to believe the fare would be mushy green beans and fried chicken. Not so. The robust and ever-changing menu offers new twists on Southern classics such as our favorite, Mississippi Mud Cake. I can't think of a more romantic place to enjoy such a rich indulgence.

Seafood Castlette

¼ cup olive oil, divided
12 large sea scallops, patted dry (about 1½ lb.)
12 peeled, jumbo raw shrimp (16/20 count)
1 lb. jumbo lump crabmeat, drained
1 cup finely chopped yellow onion
3 garlic cloves, minced
½ cup white wine
4 cups heavy cream
1 tsp. kosher salt
½ tsp. freshly ground pepper
1 (14-oz.) can quartered artichoke hearts, drained
1 bay leaf
2 cups (8 oz.) grated fresh Parmesan cheese
1 cup Japanese breadcrumbs (panko)
White truffle oil

1. Preheat broiler with oven rack 3 inches from heat. Heat 1 Tbsp. oil in a large skillet over medium-high heat. Add scallops, and cook 3 minutes on each side, adding 1 Tbsp. more oil just before turning scallops. Place 3 scallops in each of 4 individual gratin dishes.
2. Add 1 Tbsp. oil to skillet; add shrimp, and cook 2 to 3 minutes or just until shrimp turn pink. Place 3 shrimp in each gratin dish. Divide crabmeat evenly in each dish.
3. Sauté onion in 1 Tbsp. oil in skillet over medium-high heat 3 minutes or until tender. Add garlic; sauté 30 seconds. Add wine; cook 1 minute, stirring to loosen particles from skillet. Reduce heat to medium; add cream and next 4 ingredients. Simmer 5 minutes or until slightly thickened.
4. Pour 1 cup sauce over seafood. Top each with ½ cup cheese and ¼ cup breadcrumbs. Transfer to a baking sheet lined with foil; broil 2 minutes or until golden. Drizzle with oil. **Makes 4 servings.**

Mississippi Mud Cake

Cake

1 cup butter, softened
2 cups granulated sugar
4 large eggs
1 tsp. vanilla extract
1½ cups all-purpose flour
⅓ cup unsweetened cocoa
¼ tsp. salt
1 cup coarsely chopped pecans
3 cups miniature marshmallows

Icing

1½ cups powdered sugar
⅓ cup unsweetened cocoa
1 cup butter
½ cup evaporated milk
1 cup coarsely chopped pecans

1. **Prepare Cake:** Preheat oven to 350°. Beat 1 cup butter at medium speed with a mixer until creamy; gradually add sugar, beating well. Add eggs, 1 at a time, beating after each addition. Stir in vanilla.
2. Combine flour, ¼ cup cocoa, and salt; gradually add to butter mixture, beating well. Pour batter into a buttered and floured 13- x 9-inch pan. Bake at 350° for 30 to 32 minutes or until a pick inserted in center comes out clean. Sprinkle with 1 cup pecans and marshmallows. Bake 2 more minutes.
3. **Prepare Icing:** Whisk together powdered sugar and ⅓ cup cocoa. Melt 1 cup butter in a medium saucepan over medium heat. Add powdered sugar mixture and evaporated milk to melted butter, stirring until smooth. Stir in pecans. Spread half of icing over top of cake, reserving remaining icing for another use. Let cake cool completely before cutting. **Makes 12 servings.**

The Dinner Bell

McComb, Mississippi

GPS COORDINATES:
Lat./Long. 31.24079,-90.45394

229 5th Avenue 39648
(601) 684-4883
www.thedinnerbell.net

Don't Miss:

Anything

Simple Southern staples like fried chicken, chicken and dumplings, beets, green beans, and sweet tea rule the day here. The chilled banana pudding is worth the drive if you're within, oh, say four hours of McComb.

The Dinner Bell opens just for lunch, which is actually dinner. That may sound confusing if you're Southern impaired, but those from the South know that we call lunch "dinner" and dinner "supper." What? Provided you show up between 10 and 2, owner Andre Davis will seat you at a large round table for just $12.95 for an all-you-can-eat feast. However, instead of having guests trudge back and forth between a steam buffet and their seats, the Dinner Bell features giant lazy Susans on each table. Simply spin until your favorite dish is within scooping range.

Country Smothered Pork Chops

- 1   cup vegetable oil
- 1   tsp. salt
- ½   tsp. pepper
- 6   (1½-inch-thick) boneless center-cut pork chops
- 1   cup all-purpose flour
- 1   medium onion, sliced
- 3   cups chicken broth
- 2   Tbsp. cornstarch
- 2   Tbsp. browning-and-seasoning sauce
- ½   tsp. salt
- ½   tsp. garlic powder
- ½   tsp. pepper
- Hot cooked rice (optional)

1. Preheat oven to 400°. Heat oil in a large deep skillet over medium-high heat.

2. Rub 1 tsp. salt and ½ tsp. pepper all over pork chops. Dredge chops in flour, shaking off excess. Fry chops, in batches, in hot oil 2 minutes on each side. Drain on paper towels.

3. Arrange chops in a 13- x 9-inch baking dish; top with sliced onion. Combine broth and next

Rubbernecker Wonder:

Clarksdale, Mississippi

Guitar-shaped Memorial

If you haven't heard of Robert Johnson, ask any fan of the blues about the famous guitar plucker. His lonesome sounds were evidently honed in a trade with the devil right here in Clarksdale. Lucifer was hanging out at the intersection of Highways 161 and 49, in a spot now commemorated by a guitar-shaped memorial. Don't be making any deals you can't live with for eternity if you decide to visit.

5 ingredients, stirring with a whisk until blended. Pour broth mixture over chops in dish. Cover and bake at 400° for 1 hour or until chops are tender. Serve over rice, if desired. **Makes 6 servings.**

Mammy's Cupboard

Natchez, Mississippi

GPS COORDINATES:

Lat./Long. 31.488407,-91.369171

555 U.S. 61 39120

(601) 445-8957

Don't Miss:

Blueberry Lemonade

The blueberry lemonade with its surprising pinkish hue is a must. "If it gets too purple or blue," owner Lynda Moore explains, "we water it down to the perfect pink color, which means the flavor is just right too."

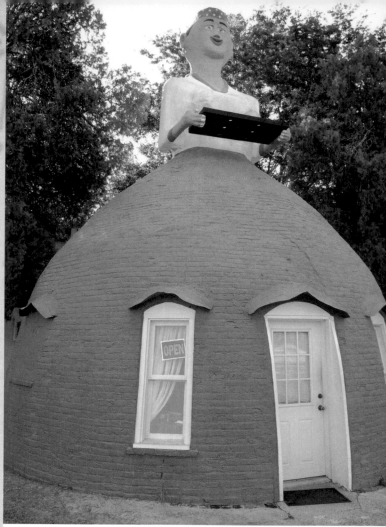

Those on the quest for good, clean gas prior to WWII often found stations shaped as dinosaurs, teepees, and gorillas. One of these roadside wonders lives on today as Mammy's Cupboard, the perfect place to grab lunch in Natchez. Once inside the painted-pink brick building shaped like a woman's skirt, you'll discover Mammy's menu loaded with sweet temptations. The breads, pies, cakes, and even lemonade are made fresh right here, making this tiny slip of a restaurant a local institution that's hard to miss. Go early—it's not unusual for Mammy's to serve 300 at lunch.

Blueberry Chutney

Ginger and garlic make this chutney a delicious addition to chicken, turkey, lamb, or pork.

4   cups fresh or frozen blueberries
¼   cup white wine vinegar
¼   cup sugar
¼   cup raisins
2   Tbsp. minced fresh ginger
2   Tbsp. minced garlic
I   Tbsp. curry powder
½   tsp. salt
I   medium onion, chopped (about 1½ cups)
¼   cup chopped fresh mint

1. Combine all ingredients, except mint, in a 2¼-qt. saucepan. Bring mixture to a boil over medium heat. Cook, stirring often, 30 minutes or until onion is tender. Remove from heat, and stir in mint.

✱ Diner Secret: Water chestnuts lend texture and pineapple adds a pleasing sweetness.

2. Ladle hot chutney into hot, sterilized jars, leaving ¼-inch headspace; wipe jar rims. Cover at once with metal lids, and screw on bands. Process in boiling water bath 10 minutes. **Makes 4 half pints.**

Mammy's Chicken Salad

2   Tbsp. salt
4   skinned, bone-in chicken breasts
I   cup mayonnaise
I   tsp. salt
I   tsp. ground ginger
I   tsp. curry powder
½   tsp. freshly ground pepper
I   cup finely chopped celery
½   cup sliced almonds
I   (8-oz.) can sliced water chestnuts, drained and cut into thin strips
I   (8-oz.) can crushed pineapple, drained

1. Bring 2 qt. water, 2 Tbsp. salt, and chicken to a boil in a large Dutch oven; reduce heat, and simmer, uncovered, 15 minutes or until chicken is tender. Remove chicken from water, and let cool 30 minutes. Bone chicken, and coarsely chop.
2. Stir together mayonnaise, 1 tsp. salt, and next 3 ingredients in a large bowl until blended. Add chicken, celery, and remaining 3 ingredients; stir well. **Makes 6 to 8 servings.**
Note: We used bone-in rather than boneless chicken breasts for more flavor.

Broccoli Cornbread

Cooking spray

6   large eggs

½   cup butter, melted

½   cup chopped onion

¼   tsp. hot sauce

l   (16-oz.) container cottage cheese

l   (8¼-oz.) can cream-style corn

4   (8.5-oz.) packages corn muffin mix

l   (10-oz.) package frozen chopped broccoli, thawed

1. Preheat oven to 350°. Coat a 13- x 9-inch pan with cooking spray.

2. Whisk eggs in a large bowl until foamy. Stir in butter and next 4 ingredients. Add muffin mix, stirring until blended.

3. Drain broccoli well, pressing between paper towels. Stir broccoli and onion into batter. (Batter will be thick.)

4. Pour batter into prepared pan. Bake at 350° for 1 hour or until bread is golden brown. **Makes 16 servings.**

✱ Diner Secret: Cottage cheese adds moisture to these towering squares, but you won't taste it.

Kentucky Bourbon Chocolate Pecan Pie

½ (14.1-oz.) package refrigerated piecrusts

1 cup sugar

1 cup light corn syrup

½ cup butter, melted

⅓ cup bourbon

1 tsp. vanilla extract

¼ tsp. salt

4 large eggs

1½ cups chopped pecans

1 cup semisweet chocolate morsels

1. Preheat oven to 350°. Fit piecrust into a 9-inch pie plate according to package directions; fold edges under, and crimp.

2. Whisk together sugar and next 6 ingredients; stir in pecans and morsels. Pour filling into prepared piecrust.

3. Bake at 350° for 1 hour and 10 minutes or until set. Let pie cool on a wire rack at least 3 hours before serving. **Makes 8 to 10 servings.**

✱ Spiked with bourbon and chocolate, pecan pie never tasted so good!

Bottletree Bakery
Oxford, Mississippi

Downtown Oxford boasts a funky bakery where you'll find suit-and-tie attorneys, students, and tourists alike. At lunchtime, order the aptly-named VanBuren Best Seller. It's piled with turkey and provolone and dressed with an Oregon raspberry mustard. The must-have item is the Apple Ruffle Tart. Owner Cynthia Gerlach and pastry chef Twinkle VanWinkle (yes, that's right) turned the basic apple tart into a work of art. Tiny rosettes of sliced Granny Smith apples are baptized in brown sugar and cinnamon and baked atop a buttery crust. Try it any day of the week except Monday (they're closed) at 923 Van Buren Avenue.

Food Find:

Mississippi

Greetings from MISSOURI

KANSAS CITY

State Capitol in Jefferson City

State Flower the Hawthorn

Bavarian influences are evident throughout this fertile region.

st Missouri Wine" 2008

M

Montelle WINERY

NG WINES

ENTRANCE

KLONDIKE CAFE

Missouri

Best Drive

Wine Country

Head west out of St. Louis on Route 94 and you'll meander over and around the Missouri River. The valley it creates is one of the prettiest you'll see in the South. The Weldon Spring Conservation Area offers hiking, fishing, and picnicking. If you're a Daniel Boone fan, you'll find his house just a few miles off the road. The quaint German town of Hermann offers old neighborhoods, excellent wineries, and unique art galleries. End your drive in stunning Rocheport, a charming town with much to explore, including the nearby Katy Trail. **Length:** 140 miles

Crown Candy Kitchen

St. Louis, Missouri

GPS COORDINATES:
Lat./Long. 38.651364,-90.197937

1401 St. Louis Avenue 63106

(314) 621-9650

www.crowncandykitchen.net

Don't Miss:

5-malt Challenge

Only take the 5-malt challenge when you're feeling really skinny. Drink five malts in 30 minutes and they're all free.

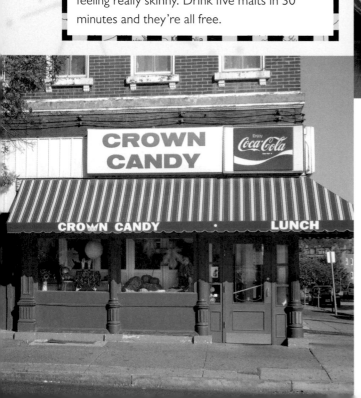

Every city needs an authentic soda shop like this. The old tin ceiling, linoleum floors, Coca-Cola memorabilia, and crooning Wurlitzer make this tiny diner the real thing. Crown Candy has been a tradition in St. Louis since 1913. Try the BLT, the egg salad sandwich, the chocolate-banana malt, or the tangy Reuben. The chocolates, rock candy, and brittles made on-site are equally delicious.

Chocolate-Banana Shake

The banana makes this shake so thick you'll get exercise trying to get it through the straw.

2   cups vanilla ice cream
¾   cup milk
⅔   cup chocolate syrup
1   banana, chopped (¾ cup)

1. Process all ingredients in a blender until smooth, stopping to scrape down sides as needed. **Makes 2 servings.**

Variation: For a malt, add 1 heaping Tbsp. of malt powder with the other ingredients, and blend until smooth.

Rubbernecker Wonder:
St. Louis, Missouri
Gateway Arch

No matter how you view it—looking up, peering down, on the spot, or from across town—the Gateway Arch says St. Louis. It's a beauty!

Grab your camera to capture the simplicity of design, silhouetted against the crisp blue sky. A gentle ray of sun ricochets off the massive curve of steel. The ride to the top changes the perspective but not the wonder.

Nearby, Laclede's Landing teems with restaurants and clubs.

When your day is done, wander back to the Arch, which glows by night, to remind you precisely where you are.

Look!

The arch gracefully frames the city from many different vantage points.

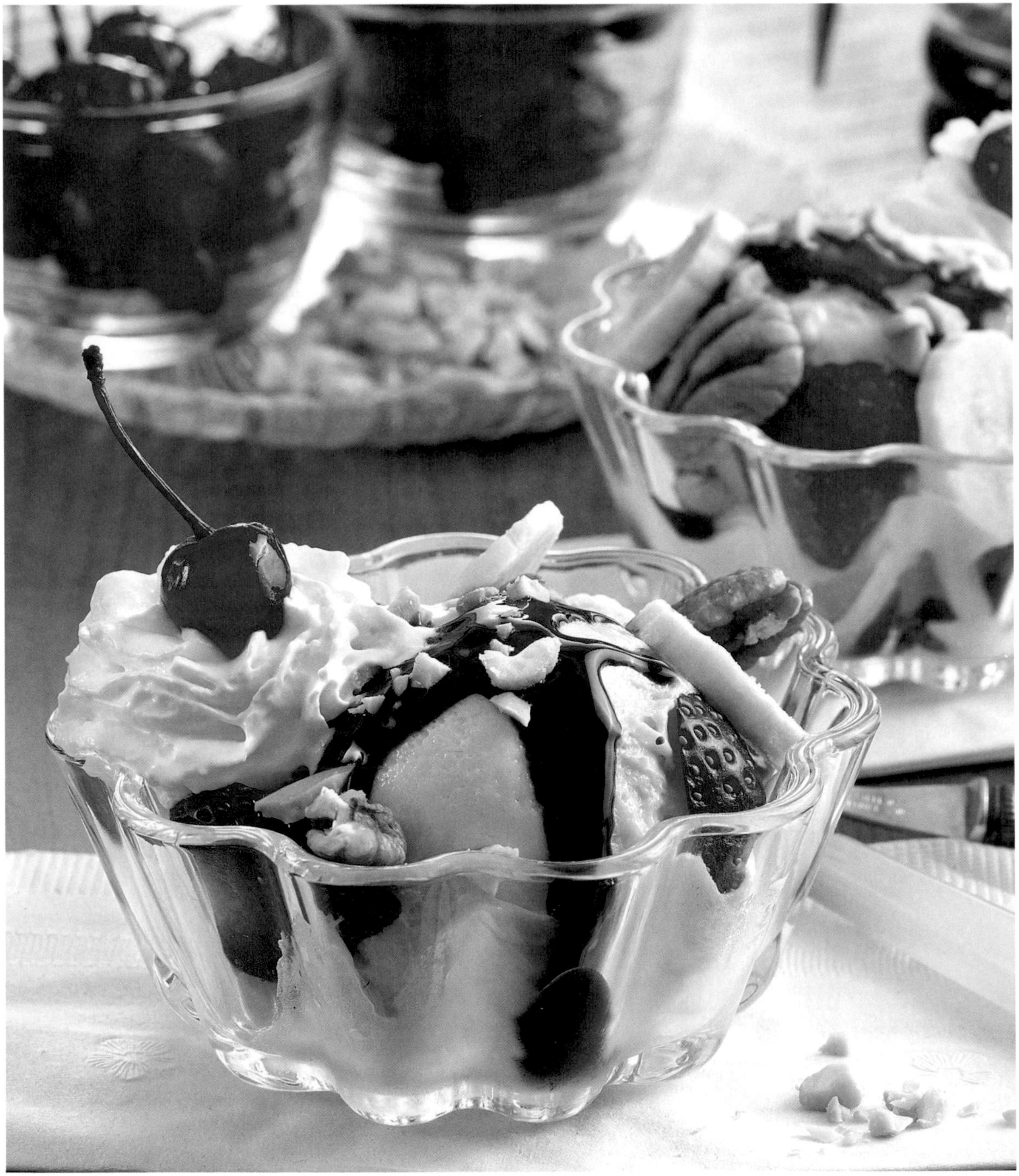

Arthur Bryant's

Kansas City, Missouri

This place serves straight up heaven on white bread, yet the decor won't inspire a sonnet. Don't go late at night. Don't expect friendly service. But there's something special about this restaurant that's woven into the fabric of this city's consciousness.

First, all great barbecue starts with the wood and the quality of the meat. Arthur Bryant's elects gorgeous cuts of ribs and giant briskets and uses fruitwood and hickory that you'd want to build furniture out of—not burn. Second, Bryant's uses double-strength pickling vinegar in the sauce, which makes for one hell of a punchy tang. Get a taste at the original location: 1727 Brooklyn Avenue.

Food Find:

Terrene

St. Louis, Missouri

GPS COORDINATES:
Lat./Long. 38.637499,-90.246622

33 North Sarah Street 63108
(314) 535-5100
www.terrene-stlouis.com

Don't Miss:

Eco-minded Touches

Chef Brian Hardesty's passion about the environment is exemplified in the restaurant's tables, which are crafted from recycled paper. Plus, the fryer oil runs a neighbor's car, and the food comes from sustainable sources.

eg
th
g
ing menu.
fries. The
and served
fare revolv
different c
on a toast
Vidalia or
menu. Ch
with ingr
pecans an

Frites and Spicy Ketchup

Serve leftover spicy ketchup with burgers or shrimp.

Spicy Ketchup

1	cup ketchup
2½	Tbsp. Dijon mustard
2	Tbsp. honey
1½	Tbsp. refrigerated horseradish
2	tsp. hot sauce
½	tsp. celery seeds
½	tsp. sherry vinegar
⅛	tsp. salt
⅛	tsp. pepper

Frites

2   lb. baking potatoes

Peanut oil

Kosher salt

Freshly ground pepper

1. Prepare Spicy Ketchup: Combine all ingredients, stirring well. Cover and chill until ready to serve.

2. Prepare Frites: Using a mandoline, cut potatoes into ⅜-inch-wide strips, leaving skins on. Soak fries in ice water for 10 minutes; drain, and pat dry.

3. Meanwhile, pour oil to depth of 3 inches into a Dutch oven; heat to 300°. Fry potatoes, in 3 batches, 4 minutes; drain on a wire rack over paper towels. Arrange potatoes on 2 large rimmed baking sheets. Freeze 1 hour.

4. Pour oil to a depth of 3 inches into a Dutch oven; heat oil to 350°. Fry potatoes, in 3 batches, 4 minutes or until golden. Drain on a wire rack over paper towels. Sprinkle lightly with kosher salt and freshly ground pepper. Serve hot with Spicy Ketchup. **Makes 4 servings.**

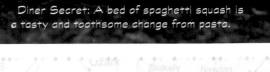

Diner Secret: A bed of spaghetti squash is a tasty and toothsome change from pasta.

Grilled Beef with Spaghetti Squash and Spinach and Mushrooms with Sage Browned Butter

Terrene's chef enjoys grilling this beef shoulder cut. We used top sirloin for convenience.

Spaghetti Squash

1	spaghetti squash (about 2½ lb.)
½	cup chicken broth
1	Tbsp. butter
¼	tsp. salt
¼	tsp. freshly ground pepper

Grilled Beef

1	lb. boneless top sirloin steak (about ¾-inch-thick)
¼	tsp. salt
½	tsp. freshly ground pepper
½	Tbsp. butter

Spinach and Mushrooms with Sage Browned Butter

2	tsp. vegetable oil
1	(3.5-oz.) package fresh shiitake mushrooms
2	tsp. butter
¼	tsp. salt
¼	tsp. freshly ground pepper
2½	(6-oz.) packages baby spinach
2	Tbsp. butter
1	Tbsp. chopped fresh sage
1½	tsp. fresh lemon juice

1. **Prepare Spaghetti Squash:** Preheat oven to 350°. Cut squash in half lengthwise, and remove seeds. Place squash, cut sides down, on an aluminum foil–lined baking sheet. Bake, uncovered, at 350° for 45 minutes or until tender; let stand 10 minutes. Remove spaghetti-like strands with a fork, discarding shells.

2. Combine squash and broth in a large skillet. Cook over medium-high heat 3 to 4 minutes or until most of liquid evaporates. Add 1 Tbsp. butter and ¼ tsp. each salt and pepper. Stir just until butter melts. Cover and set aside.

3. **Prepare Grilled Beef:** Preheat grill to 400° to 450° (high) heat. Sprinkle steak with ¼ tsp. salt and ½ tsp. pepper. Grill, covered with grill lid, 5 minutes on each side or to desired degree of doneness. Remove steaks from grill; rub with ½ Tbsp. butter, and cover with aluminum foil.

4. **Meanwhile, prepare Spinach and Mushrooms with Sage Browned Butter:** Heat oil in a large skillet over medium-high heat. Add mushrooms and next 3 ingredients; sauté 2 minutes. Gradually add spinach; cook 2 to 3 minutes or until spinach is wilted.

5. Cook 2 Tbsp. butter in a saucepan over medium heat 1 to 2 minutes or just until butter starts to brown. Remove from heat; stir in sage and lemon juice.

6. Cut steak across the grain into ½-inch slices; arrange on serving plates over mounds of squash and sautéed spinach and mushroom mixture. Drizzle each serving with sage butter. **Makes 4 servings.**

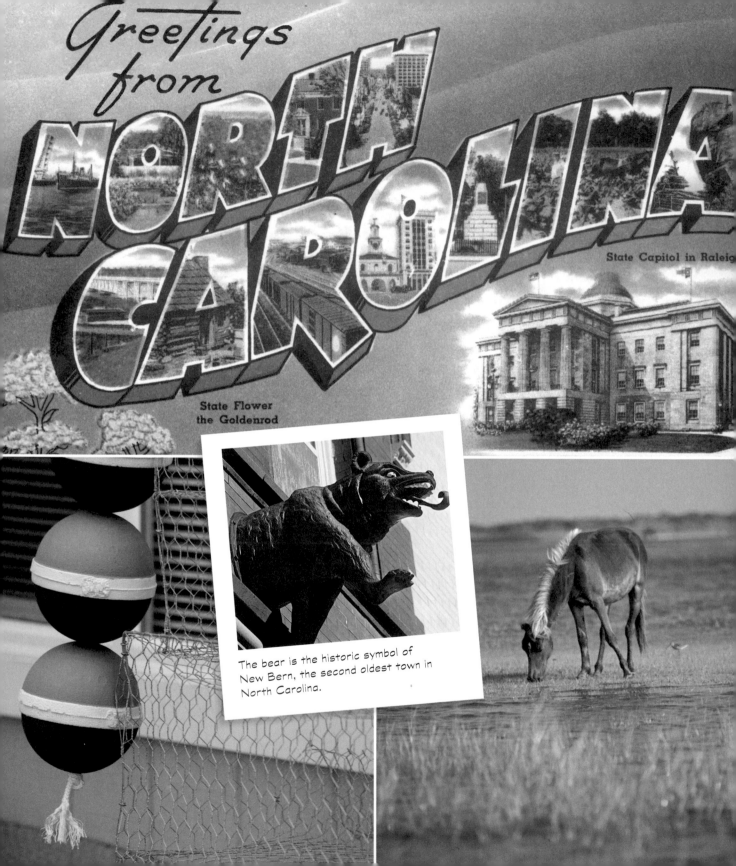

Greetings from

NORTH CAROLINA

State Capitol in Raleig

State Flower
the Goldenrod

The bear is the historic symbol of
New Bern, the second oldest town in
North Carolina.

North Carolina

Best Drive

The Outer Banks

Measure your next road trip along North Carolina's famed Outer Banks by lighthouses. Yes, lighthouses. There are six to visit along this treacherous but stunning coast. The Currituck Beach Light Station was opened in 1875 and contains one-million bricks. Cruise down Highway 12 past Kitty Hawk (a great spot to stop for some flying history) and you'll come upon the Bodie Island Lighthouse. Standing 156 feet high, its black-and-white stripes can be seen from 19 miles away. Okracoke, another 70 miles south, offers a mix of wild horses, charming restaurants, and beautiful homes. Stop by the nearby Cape Hatteras Lighthouse, which sports a green light. And the Okracoke Lighthouse is still in active service. Though relatively short, it has the benefit of being in the middle of this wonderful beachfront town.

Length: 147 miles

Crook's Corner

Chapel Hill, North Carolina

GPS COORDINATES:
Lat./Long. 35.909668,-79.065007

610 West Franklin Street 27516
(919) 926-7643
www.crookscorner.com

Don't Miss:

Shrimp and Grits

The most famous dish at Crook's Corner has to be the shrimp and grits: a creamy, crunchy marvel. Have it with the mint julep sorbet, and life doesn't get much better.

Located in a bend and concealed behind a thicket festooned with hubcaps and crowned by a pig that looks fresh from its buttermilk bath for the State Fair, Crook's Corner has all the hallmarks of a Southern dive. Don't fall for it, though. Inside you'll find a gourmet menu that celebrates the very finest of our region's cuisine. The menu changes nightly, and chef Bill Smith has a gift for playful new twists on some of your favorite standbys.

Mint Syrup

This is a simple thing they do at Crook's Corner, but people ask for this recipe as much as they do for any other. It's a syrup that they invented in order to serve both sweetened and unsweetened tea without having to take up counter space for two separate vats.

2   cups sugar
2   cups tightly packed fresh mint
1   tsp. lemon zest
¾   cup fresh lemon juice

1. Bring sugar and 2 cups water to a boil in a non-aluminum saucepan. Cook, stirring constantly, until sugar dissolves. Remove from heat; stir in mint leaves and lemon zest. Cover tightly, and steep 15 minutes.
2. Strain mint mixture into a pitcher, discarding solids. Add lemon juice to pitcher. Cover and chill at least 2 hours. **Makes 4 cups.**
Note: To make sorbet, double the entire recipe (except for the sugar which remains at 2 cups). Chill syrup at least 2 hours before freezing in the ice-cream maker according to manufacturer's directions. Serve immediately, or freeze 2 hours until firm.

✱ Diner Secret: Make other sorbets, like basil, using this same method.

Green Tabasco Chicken

Chef Bill Smith prefers roasted chicken to be a little past done; it will be better cold the next day, if there is any left.

1	(4-lb.) whole chicken
1	tsp. salt
½	tsp. freshly ground pepper
1	lemon, halved
1	jalapeño pepper, halved
1	garlic clove, peeled and halved

Kitchen string

⅓	cup green hot sauce
¼	tsp. salt
¼	tsp. freshly ground pepper
½	cup butter, melted
1½	cups dry white wine

1. Preheat oven to 500°. Rinse chicken, and pat dry. Using kitchen shears, snip off the pope's nose (see last Note below, right) and the last joint of each chicken wing. Set aside. Sprinkle chicken cavity with 1 tsp. salt and ½ tsp. pepper; squeeze lemon into cavity, and stuff cavity with lemon, jalapeño, and garlic halves. Tie chicken legs together with kitchen string; tuck wings under, and place on a rack in a lightly greased roasting pan. Baste chicken with hot sauce; sprinkle with ¼ tsp. each salt and pepper.

2. Bake chicken at 500° for 20 minutes; reduce oven temperature to 350°, and continue to bake 55 more minutes or until a thermometer inserted in the breast registers 170° and chicken is done, basting every 20 minutes with melted butter.

3. Meanwhile, place reserved pope's nose, wingtips, and giblets (except liver) in a 1-qt. saucepan; cover with cold water. Bring to a boil; reduce heat, and simmer, uncovered, 1 hour.

4. Let roasted chicken rest 20 minutes or until cool to the touch; remove and discard string. Using kitchen shears, cut out the spine, reserving juices from cavity. Place spine, chicken juices, jalapeño, and garlic from cavity into 1-qt. saucepan with giblets (discarding lemon); bring to a boil over high heat. Cook 2 minutes; remove from heat, and strain.

5. Cut roasted chicken into serving-size pieces; place on a serving platter; cover and keep warm.

6. Meanwhile, place roasting pan across 2 stovetop burners over high heat. Add wine, stirring to loosen particles from bottom of pan. Add strained broth mixture to pan. Cook, uncovered, 10 minutes or until sauce is reduced and thickened. Remove from heat; strain sauce. Drizzle desired amount of sauce over chicken on platter. Serve with remaining sauce. **Makes 4 servings.**

Note: The term "pope's nose" refers to the tail of the chicken at one end of the spine.

The Ham Shoppe

Valle Crucis, North Carolina

GPS COORDINATES:

Lat./Long. 36.19411,-81.745634

124 Broadstone Road 28691

(828) 963-6310

www.thehamshoppeandmore.com

Don't Miss:

Dena

Dena makes all of the pies at The Ham Shoppe. She recommends a heavy egg wash to give your slice of heaven a shiny brown crust. This extra step will wow your guests.

* Diner Secret: A splash of jalapeño pepper juice adds a zesty punch to pimiento cheese.

I n this crook in the road, you'll find a country store full of surprises. Sure, there's the usual assortment of general store honey, jams, and jellies. But gourmands visit for the elegant twists on Southern classics such as pimiento cheese (twinged with a bit of jalapeño), rhubarb pie (tart enough to make your eyelids flutter), and sandwiches made with freshly-baked bread and seasonal organic ingredients. There's no place to sit inside, so you'll have to eat your egg, chicken, or ham salad on the hood of your car.

The Caitlin

You can spread any extra pimiento cheese filling on crackers or celery sticks.

4   oz. pepper Jack cheese
4   oz. Cheddar cheese
4   oz. Swiss cheese
4   oz. Havarti cheese
¼   cup pickled jalapeño pepper juice
¼   cup mayonnaise
2   (8-oz.) packages cream cheese, softened
2   (4-oz.) jars diced pimientos, drained
16   sourdough bread slices, toasted
½   cup tightly packed baby spinach leaves
1½   cups thin cucumber slices
1   cup thin onion slices
½   cup alfalfa sprouts
8   cooked bacon slices

1. Position shredding disk in food processor bowl; shred first 4 ingredients, and place in a large bowl. Add pepper juice and next 3 ingredients; stir well.
2. Spread ½ cup pimiento cheese filling on each of 8 toast slices. Top pimiento cheese evenly with spinach leaves, cucumber slices, onion slices, alfalfa sprouts, bacon slices, and remaining toast slices. **Makes 8 servings.**

White Beans and Ham

¼   cup butter
1½   cups chopped cooked ham
1   cup chopped onion
4   garlic cloves, minced
½   tsp. onion salt
¼   tsp. ground cumin
¼   cup minced fresh parsley
2   (15.8-oz.) Great Northern beans, undrained

1. Melt butter in a large saucepan over medium heat. Add cooked ham, onion, and garlic; sauté 5 minutes. Stir in ¾ cup water, onion salt, and remaining ingredients. Bring to a boil; cover, reduce heat, and simmer 5 minutes, stirring occasionally. Serve with a square of cornbread. **Makes about 6 cups.**

Strawberry-Rhubarb Pie

1 cup sugar

5 Tbsp. cornstarch

¼ tsp. ground nutmeg

3 cups fresh or frozen rhubarb slices, thawed and drained

2 cups sliced fresh strawberries

½ (14.1-oz.) package refrigerated piecrusts

2 Tbsp. butter, cut into small pieces

1 large egg, beaten

1. Preheat oven to 350°. Whisk together first 3 ingredients in a large bowl until blended. Add rhubarb and strawberries, tossing to coat. Set aside.

2. Fit piecrust into a 9-inch pie plate according to package directions; fold edges under, and crimp. Spoon rhubarb mixture into prepared crust; dot with butter. Brush edges of crust with beaten egg.

3. Bake at 350° for 1 hour. Let cool completely on a wire rack. **Makes 8 servings.**

Penguin's Drive-In
Charlotte, North Carolina

This Charlotte institution began life as an ice-cream parlor, hence the penguin. Today the popular restaurant serves up tremendous burgers, hot dogs, soups, and fries, with a serious dose of cool. Patrons begin lining up at the small dining room's front door before it opens, so get there early. Try the grilled pimiento cheese, super-juicy Big Block Burger, or sweet banana pudding. Then waddle out like a penguin. 1921 Commonwealth Ave.

Sometimes you want honey-glazed ham and sometimes just honey. You can take your pick here.

Food Find:

The Jarrett House

Dillsboro, North Carolina

GPS COORDINATES:
Lat./Long. 35.379591,-83.264861

100 Haywood Road 28725

(828) 586-0265

www.jarretthouse.com

Don't Miss:

Chicken and Dumplings

I'd be a dumpling myself if I lived anywhere near the Jarrett House since I find their chicken and dumplings truly irresistible. And if you're wondering about the vinegar pie recipe featured here, give it a try. The taste is something between a poundcake and a pecan pie without pecans. Yum.

Supper at Grandmama's house, dinner after a church service, or Thanksgiving on the farm—a meal at the historical Jarrett House feels like all of these. Dishes such as pot roast, fried chicken, green beans, candied apples, and baby carrots are served in huge portions for the table to share. The cooking here is as straightforward and simple as their buttery biscuits. You won't find complex ingredients or cutting-edge techniques. But what you will find is delectable Southern fare served with a smile.

* Diner Secret: Two kinds of pepper give this homey dish a country kick.

Chicken and Dumplings

Chicken

1	(5-lb.) cut-up whole chicken
¼	cup chopped fresh parsley
1	Tbsp. jarred chicken soup base
1	Tbsp. butter
½	tsp. salt
¼	tsp. black pepper
½	tsp. crushed red pepper

Dumplings

3	Tbsp. shortening
2	cups self-rising flour
⅓	cup milk
¼	cup buttermilk

1. **Prepare Chicken:** Bring chicken and 3½ qt. water to a boil in an 8-qt. stockpot; cover, reduce heat, and simmer 25 minutes or until tender.
2. Remove chicken from pan, reserving 10 cups broth. Skin and bone chicken. Shred chicken to measure 4½ cups; set aside.

3. **Prepare Dumplings:** Cut shortening into flour with a pastry blender or fork until crumbly. Add milks, stirring just until dry ingredients are moistened. Turn dough out onto a lightly floured surface, and knead lightly 5 or 6 times. Roll out dough to a 14- x 10-inch rectangle. Cut dough into about 1-inch squares. Let dumplings stand, uncovered, 5 minutes.
4. Meanwhile, combine reserved broth, parsley and next 5 ingredients in Dutch oven. Bring to a boil; reduce heat to a simmer. Drop dumplings into simmering broth. Cook 8 minutes or until tender, stirring gently twice. Gently stir in chicken. Cook 2 minutes or until thoroughly heated. Remove from heat, and let stand 10 minutes before serving. **Makes 8 servings.**

Jarrett House Vinegar Pie

½	(14.1-oz.) package refrigerated piecrusts
3	large eggs
1½	cups sugar
½	cup butter, melted and cooled
2	Tbsp. all-purpose flour
2	Tbsp. cider vinegar
1	Tbsp. vanilla extract

1. Preheat oven to 325°. Unroll piecrust. Fit into a 9-inch pie plate; fold edges under, and crimp.
2. Whisk together eggs and remaining ingredients in a medium bowl. Pour filling into prepared piecrust.
3. Bake at 325° for 50 minutes or until set and golden brown. Cool completely on a wire rack. **Makes 8 servings.**

* Diner Secret: Self-rising flour gives you a leg up when preparing these easy, four-ingredient biscuits.

Jarrett House Biscuits

⅓ cup shortening
2 cups self-rising flour
⅓ cup milk
⅓ cup buttermilk

1. Preheat oven to 450°. Cut shortening into flour with a pastry blender or fork until crumbly. Add milks, stirring just until dry ingredients are moistened.
2. Turn dough out onto a lightly floured surface, and knead lightly 3 or 4 times. Pat or roll dough to ¾-inch thickness; cut dough with a 2½-inch round cutter, and place dough rounds ½ inch apart on an ungreased baking sheet.
3. Bake at 450° for 12 minutes or until golden brown. **Makes 8 servings.**

Jarrett House Apples

2 lb. apples, peeled and sliced
1 cup sugar

1. Combine apple slices, sugar, and ¼ cup water in a large skillet. Cover apple mixture and cook over medium-high heat 12 minutes. Uncover and cook, stirring often, 6 to 8 minutes or until glazed. **Makes 6 servings.**

Okie Dokies Smokehouse

Swannanoa, North Carolina

GPS COORDINATES:

Lat./Long. 35.600439, -82.400908

2375 U.S. Highway 70 28778

(828) 686-0050

www.okiedokiesbbq.com

Don't Miss:

Hush Puppies

When Okie Dokies' basket of hot, fresh hush puppies arrives at your table, resist the temptation to scarf them all down. Their jalapeño hotness has a way of catching up with you.

Vary your sauce options. Stir wing sauce to taste into the Ranch dressing.

My shipmate in the Navy told me about this heavenly barbecue stop near Asheville. Trust a naval officer to hunt down the best chow around. Okie Dokies ranks as championship 'que. The pork is the juiciest I've ever tasted. This swine dining establishment prides itself on its sides—mac and cheese, collard greens, baked beans, fried dill pickles, and two kinds of slaw will vie for your attention.

Crispy Fried Pickles

4   cups dill pickle chips, drained
1½   cups 1.5% low-fat buttermilk
½   cup Ranch dressing
2   Tbsp. mild barbecue sauce
Canola oil
4   cups all-purpose flour
2   Tbsp. barbecue seasoning

1. Place pickle chips in a large bowl. Pour buttermilk over chips. Cover and chill 1 hour.
2. Meanwhile, stir together the dressing and barbecue sauce in a small bowl. Cover and chill until ready to serve.
3. Pour oil to a depth of 1½ inches into a large deep skillet. Heat over high heat to 375°.
4. Meanwhile, pour pickle mixture through a strainer over a bowl, discarding buttermilk. Whisk together flour and barbecue seasoning in a large bowl until blended.

✱ Diner Secret: Two kinds of pepper give this homey dish a country kick.

5. Add half of pickles to flour mixture, tossing to coat; remove pickles from flour mixture with a slotted spoon, shaking off excess. Fry pickles 3 to 4 minutes or until golden. Drain on paper towels. Repeat procedure with remaining pickles and flour mixture. Serve pickles with sauce. **Makes 8 to 10 servings.**

Jalapeño Hush Puppies

Vegetable oil
2   cups yellow cornmeal
1   cup all-purpose flour
½   cup sugar
3   Tbsp. dried minced onion
½   tsp. Creole seasoning
¼   tsp. salt
¼   tsp. baking soda
2   large eggs
⅔   cup instant nonfat dry milk
3   Tbsp. white vinegar
8   medium jalapeño peppers, seeded
     and chopped (1 cup)

1. Pour vegetable oil to depth of 2 inches into a Dutch oven. Heat to 375° over medium–high heat.
2. Meanwhile, stir together cornmeal and next 6 ingredients. Whisk together eggs, 1¼ cups water, milk powder, and vinegar; add to dry mixture, stirring just until moistened. Stir in jalapeños. Drop batter by rounded tablespoon into hot oil, and fry, in batches, 3 minutes or until golden, turning once. Drain on a wire rack over paper towels. **Makes about 3½ dozen.**

Poole's Downtown Diner

Raleigh, North Carolina

Lat./Long. 35.774718,-78.642304

426 South McDowell Street 27601

(919) 832-4477

www.poolesdowntowndiner.com

Don't Miss:

The Warning Sign

The original owners of Poole's Downtown Diner posted a small sign that read, "If you don't use profanity, you won't offend anyone." If you look carefully on the back wall you'll see that original message continues to grace the restaurant.

* Diner Secret: Sherry, cream and butter elevate this from diner to fine-dining fare.

Luncheon stools and curved counters still fill this evolved eatery, but the big-haired waitresses and bad coffee linger on only in pictures. Poole's is no ordinary diner. Open only for dinner, its trendy bar scene and ever-changing menu create a distinctly hip vibe. Check out the chalkboard and order up a classic such as beet salad or peach cobbler.

Roasted Brussels Sprouts and Oyster Mushrooms with Sherry

A sizzling hot skillet ensures a good sear on these sprouts; then cream and sherry add richness.

½ lb. fresh Brussels sprouts
2 (3.5-oz.) packages fresh oyster mushrooms
3 Tbsp. canola oil, divided
½ tsp. kosher salt, divided
¼ cup dry sherry
½ cup heavy cream
2 Tbsp. butter
2 tsp. fresh lemon juice
¼ tsp. freshly ground pepper

1. Remove discolored leaves from Brussels sprouts. Cut off stem ends, and thinly slice sprouts. Remove and discard mushroom stems. Cut mushrooms into 2-inch pieces.
2. Heat 2 Tbsp. oil in a large skillet or sauté pan over medium-high heat. Add mushrooms; cook 4 minutes (do not stir). Turn mushrooms, and cook 1 more minute or until browned and crisp. Sprinkle with ¼ tsp. salt. Remove from heat; transfer mushrooms to a small bowl.
3. Heat 1 Tbsp. oil in skillet over medium-high heat. Add Brussels sprouts; sauté 4 minutes or until tender. Sprinkle with ¼ tsp. salt. Add sherry, and cook 2 minutes, stirring to loosen particles from bottom of skillet. Add cream; cook over medium-high heat 1 minute or until slightly thickened. Add butter, 1 Tbsp. at a time, stirring until butter melts after each addition. Add reserved mushrooms; cook 30 seconds or just until thoroughly heated. Remove from heat; stir in lemon juice and pepper. **Makes 4 servings.**

Watermelon Salad with Chèvre, Basil, and Vidalia Onion-Champagne Vinaigrette

In the peak of summer, sliced watermelon sprinkled with cheese and basil is an absolute treat.

1 (7- to 8-lb.) small ripe watermelon
2 Tbsp. extra virgin olive oil
¼ tsp. sea salt
½ tsp. freshly ground pepper
1 (4-oz.) goat cheese log, crumbled
½ cup chopped fresh basil
Vinaigrette

1. Cut watermelon into quarters; slice into 1½-inch slabs, and remove rind. Arrange melon on a serving platter. Drizzle with oil; sprinkle with salt and pepper. Sprinkle with crumbled cheese and basil; drizzle with vinaigrette. **Makes 10 to 12 servings.**
Note: We tested with a Sugar Baby Watermelon.

Vidalia Onion-Champagne Vinaigrette

½ cup minced Vidalia onion
¼ cup Champagne vinegar
1 Tbsp. honey
⅛ tsp. sea salt
½ cup canola oil

1. Combine onion and vinegar in a 2-cup glass measuring cup; let stand 5 minutes. Whisk in honey and sea salt. Gradually add oil in a slow steady stream, whisking constantly. **Makes 1 cup.**

Rubbernecker Wonder:
Mount Airy, North Carolina
Andy Griffith's Hometown

If you've wanted to carry a bullet or set up Checkpoint Chickie, drop by Squad Car Tours here in Mount Airy. For just $30, you can see Andy Griffith's hometown from the camp confines of a vintage patrol car. Tours run daily. Go to www.visitmayberry.com for information.

Honk your horn and tell Goober or Gomer you need a fill up.

Snappy Lunch

Mount Airy, North Carolina

GPS COORDINATES:

Lat./Long. 36.4997,-80.607343

125 North Main Street 27030

(336) 786-4931

Don't Miss:

Being a Regular

If you really want to feel like a regular, park it in the old wooden booths of the front section, grab a newspaper, and settle in with one of Snappy Lunch's excellent cups of coffee.

Andy, Opie, and Barnie made Mount Airy famous, but Snappy Lunch has been feeding Mayberry fans for generations. Its famous concoction, the Pork Chop Sandwich, may be the messiest pork dish in North Carolina. A fried pork tenderloin topped with chili, slaw, lettuce, and tomato oozes flavor with every bite. Have it with some chips, and wash it down with a cool chocolate milk. Nothing gets more Mayberry than this.

* Diner Secret: If desired, top this tender pork sandwich with your favorite chili.

Pork Chop Sandwich

10 (3½-oz.) boneless pork loin chops
Vegetable oil
1 cup all-purpose flour
1 Tbsp. sugar
½ tsp. salt
1 large egg
⅔ cup milk
5 large hamburger buns
Yellow mustard
10 tomato slices
Coleslaw

1. Place pork between 2 sheets of plastic wrap, and flatten to ¼-inch thickness, using a rolling pin or flat side of a meat mallet.
2. Pour oil to a depth of 1 inch in a large skillet; heat over medium-high heat to 375°.
3. Meanwhile, combine flour, sugar, and salt in a medium bowl. Stir together egg and milk; add to dry mixture, beating until smooth. Dip pork, in batches, into batter, and fry 3 minutes on each side or until golden and pork is done. Drain on a wire rack over paper towels.
4. Spread both halves of each bun with desired amount of mustard. Layer with 2 pork chops, 2 tomato slices, and desired amount of coleslaw on bottom half of each bun. Cover with top halves of buns. **Makes 5 servings.**

Coleslaw

1 cup mayonnaise
¼ cup sugar
¼ cup white vinegar
½ head cabbage, finely chopped (7½ cups)
¼ cup finely chopped carrot
¼ cup finely chopped green bell pepper

1. Stir together first 3 ingredients in a large bowl. Add cabbage and remaining ingredients, stirring well. Cover and chill until ready to serve. **Makes 12 servings.**

As long as nobody's watching, I'll have myself a nibble.

Oklahoma

Best Drive

Route 66

Of all the states that boast segments of America's most famous highway, Oklahoma may indeed have the best-preserved remnants of the old road. The state certainly has the best kitschy stuff, such as the Round Barn, Totem Pole Park, Rock Cafe, and the Blue Whale, to name a few. Much of the original two-lane tarmac remains, which makes drivers feel like they've motored straight back to 1930. Sure, the state has a lot of flat (and I mean FLAT) scenery, but it's the kind of cool American highway that lures visitors from around the world. Since much of the original road is gone, make sure to plan your trip in advance. The Oklahoma Route 66 Association is a great resource at www.oklahomaroute66.com.
Length: varies

Oklahoma

Brothers Houligan

Tulsa, Oklahoma

GPS COORDINATES:
Lat./Long. 36.140522,-95.955708

2508 East 15th Street 74104
(918) 747-1086
www.broshouligan.com

Don't Miss:

Cottage Fries

What are cottage fries? Certainly not some wispy French fry, that's for sure. The Brothers Houligan cottage fry is a meal unto itself. It's big, chunky, and shaped like a waffle. This is a serious fry, perfectly made to soak up its condiment companion, gravy. Oh yeah, you read that right: gravy. Blam!

If you find yourself wandering the west, a natural and altogether fitting thing to do is to saunter into a saloon. Now, you might think a bar won't have great food, and in most cases you'd be right. As befits a watering hole, Brothers Houligan has the typical burgers, fries, etc. But delve a tad deeper on the menu and check out the chicken-fried steak. How can you go wrong with a deep-fried slab o' meat doused in white gravy? You can't. Which is why I'm telling you to eat it. You'll thank me later.

* Diner Secret: Southern cooks know bacon makes everything better.

Green Beans

4	bacon slices
½	cup chopped white onion
2	tsp. seasoned salt
1	(16-oz.) package frozen French-cut green beans

1. Preheat oven to 350°. Cook bacon in a large skillet over medium-high heat 7 minutes or until crisp; remove, and drain on paper towels, reserving drippings in skillet. Crumble bacon.

2. Sauté onion in hot drippings 3 minutes or until tender. Remove from heat; stir in seasoned salt and green beans. Spoon green bean mixture into a lightly greased 8-inch square baking dish; sprinkle with bacon.

3. Bake, uncovered, at 350° for 45 minutes or until thoroughly heated. **Makes 4 servings.**

Rubbernecker Wonder:

Foyil, Oklahoma

1940s Totem Pole

It's not the tallest totem pole, nor is it made out of wood. And the carver, Ed Galloway, wasn't a Native American. No matter. This giant tribute to American folk art, completed in the late 1940s, is a colorful piece of highway Americana worth the slight detour off historic Route 66. Today, it sits on the National Register of Historic Places.

One man's art is now a nation's roadside treasure.

Look!

* Diner Secret: Chili powder gives this crunchy coating a kick!

Chicken-Fried Steak

Serve these tender, crusty steaks with cream gravy over a pile of mashed potatoes.

3½ cups peanut oil
1 cup all-purpose flour
1½ Tbsp. seasoned salt
2 tsp. freshly ground pepper
2 tsp. chili powder
¾ cup milk
2 large eggs
4 (4-oz.) cubed steaks
Country Gravy

1. Pour oil into a 12-inch skillet; heat to 360°.
2. Meanwhile, combine flour, salt, pepper, and chili powder. Whisk together milk and eggs. Dredge steaks in flour mixture, shaking off excess. Dip steaks in milk mixture, and heavily dredge again in flour mixture.
3. Fry steaks 2 to 3 minutes on each side or until golden brown. Drain on paper towels. Serve with Country Gravy. **Makes 4 servings.**

Country Gravy

⅓ cup instant nonfat dry milk
1 tsp. jarred chicken soup base
⅛ tsp. freshly ground pepper
1 (2.64-oz.) envelope country gravy mix

1. Combine all ingredients in a small saucepan; whisk in 2 cups water. Bring to a boil over medium heat, stirring frequently; reduce heat, and simmer 1 minute, stirring constantly. Remove from heat; serve with Chicken-Fried Steak. **Makes 2¼ cups.**

Rubbernecker Wonder:

Stockyards City, Oklahoma

Where Dudes Get Duds

Rooted in pioneer history, Stockyards City feels like a Wild West wonderland. It's loaded with some of the fanciest Western-wear outfitters in the country. Arrive in street duds and by high noon look like either Garth Brooks or Carrie Underwood.

Shorty's Caboy Hattery
1206 South Agnew Avenue;
www.shortyshattery.com or (405) 232-4287

Little Joes Boots
2219 Exchange Avenue;
www.littlejoesboots.net or (405) 236-2650

Langston's
2224 Exchange Avenue;
www.langstons.com or (405) 235-9536

Hey, over here...check out the best cowboy duds west of the Mississippi.

Look!

Cattlemen's Steakhouse

Oklahoma City, Oklahoma

GPS COORDINATES:
Lat./Long. 35.452373,-97.555016

1309 South Agnew Avenue 73108
(405) 236-0416
www.cattlemensrestaurant.com

Don't Miss:

The Ripe Aroma

…even if you wish you could! Road food acolytes know a giant, reeking stockyard next to a restaurant that's bustling with truckers, cowboys, and our bovine friends means you're in a great place for steak.

The doors open at 6 a.m., and I'm not ashamed to tell you that I've been there at that hour to chow down on a big honking T-bone and coconut pie. And my cheery waitress didn't bat one of her heavily-mascaraed eyelashes at my order. Why? Because this is the best damned steakhouse in the country. Period. Heaven will have a salty, tender, and perfectly cooked Cattlemen's steak waiting on me if I make it through the Pearly Gates. Somebody put a steak knife in my casket.

Coconut Cream Pie

- ½ (14.1-oz.) package refrigerated piecrusts
- ⅔ cup sugar
- 3 Tbsp. cornstarch
- ¼ tsp. salt
- 2½ cups milk
- 2 egg yolks, beaten
- ⅓ cup butter
- ½ tsp. vanilla
- 1⅓ cups sweetened flaked coconut
- 4 egg whites
- ¼ tsp. cream of tartar
- ½ cup sugar
- 1 Tbsp. sweetened flaked coconut

1. Preheat oven to 450°. Fit piecrust into a 9-inch pie plate according to package directions; fold edges under, and crimp. Prick bottom and sides of piecrust with a fork. Bake at 450° for 10 minutes or until golden brown. Set piecrust aside on a wire rack while preparing filling. Reduce oven temperature to 325°.

2. Combine sugar, cornstarch, and salt in a medium saucepan. Gradually stir in milk. Cook, stirring constantly, over medium-high heat until mixture comes to a boil; boil, stirring constantly, 1 minute. Remove from heat. Gradually stir about one-fourth of hot milk mixture into yolks; add yolk mixture to remaining hot milk mixture, stirring constantly. Cook, stirring constantly, over medium heat 3 minutes. Remove from heat, and add butter and vanilla, stirring until butter melts. Stir in 1⅓ cups coconut. Cover and keep warm.

3. Beat egg whites and cream of tartar at high speed with an electric mixer until foamy. Gradually add ½ cup sugar, 1 Tbsp. at a time, beating until stiff peaks form and sugar dissolves. Sprin-

kle 1 Tbsp. coconut in bottom of piecrust. Pour hot filling over coconut. Spread meringue over filling, sealing edges.

4. Bake at 325° for 20 to 25 minutes or until golden brown. Let pie cool completely on a wire rack. **Makes 8 servings.**

Peppercorn Sauce

- 2 tsp. jarred beef soup base
- 2 cups hot water
- 2 Tbsp. butter
- 2½ Tbsp. all-purpose flour
- ½ cup plus 2 Tbsp. crème fraîche
- 1 Tbsp. brandy
- 2¼ tsp. coarse black pepper

1. Dissolve soup base in hot water to make a broth. Melt butter in a saucepan over medium heat. Whisk in flour; cook, whisking constantly until golden brown. Slowly whisk in warm broth. Cook, whisking constantly, 5 minutes or until thickened. Whisk in crème fraîche, brandy, and pepper. **Makes 2¼ cups**

* Diner Secret: Crème fraîche delivers uncommon richness to this country-style gravy.

Lucille's Roadhouse

Weatherford, Oklahoma

GPS COORDINATES:

Lat./Long. 35.542958,-98.658726

1301 North Airport Road 73096

(580) 772-8808

Don't Miss:

The Fried Onion Burger

Have a little crunch with your beef. Finish it off with some apple fritters for a meal straight from 1959. That's a good thing.

I f the word "roadhouse" conjures images of gas pumps, pot roast, and vinyl barstools, then you already know what to expect when you pull into Lucille's. And doesn't "Lucille" just make you think of the fifties? If not, you got some splanin' to do. The restaurant's simple American menu (burgers, fries, and lots more delicious fried stuff) fits its Route 66 origins. Once a gas station (down the road apiece), Lucille's no longer pumps gas. But if it's a hot day and you're in the mood for a cold beer, you'll find three Oklahoma brews on tap. This roadhouse remains a comfort-food heaven and an excellent place to pick up the flavor of America's mother road.

Lucille's coffee with Sunday Apple Fritters are like an Okie's beignets and chicory.

Sunday Apple Fritters

Fry up these light dessert fritters in the fall when apples are at their peak.

Canola oil

2   cups all-purpose flour
⅔   cup sugar
1½   tsp. baking powder
1   tsp. salt
2   large apples, unpeeled and finely chopped (about 3 cups)
⅔   cup milk
2   tsp. vanilla extract
2   large eggs
Powdered sugar

1. Pour oil to depth of 2 inches into a Dutch oven; heat to 350°. Combine flour and next 3 ingredients. Stir in chopped apple, tossing gently to coat. Make a well in center of mixture.
2. Whisk together milk, vanilla, and eggs until blended. Add to flour mixture, stirring just until dry ingredients are moistened.

3. Drop batter by heaping Tbsp. into hot oil. Fry fritters in batches, 1 to 2 minutes on each side or until golden. Drain on paper towels. Sprinkle fritters with powdered sugar. **Makes 3 dozen.** **Note:** We tested with Braeburn apples.

Lucille's Pot Roast

Enjoy this classic slow-cooker pot roast flavored with onion soup mix and beer.

2   small onions, cut into quarters
1½   lb. new potatoes, halved
1   lb. carrots, cut into 3-inch pieces
1   (4- to 5-lb.) boneless beef rump roast
2   tsp. sugar
1   tsp. dried oregano
½   tsp. salt
½   tsp. pepper
2   (10½-oz.) cans condensed beef broth
1   (12-oz.) bottle beer
1   (1-oz.) envelope dry onion soup mix
2   garlic cloves, minced

1. Combine onions, potatoes, and carrots in a 6-qt. slow cooker. Place roast over vegetables in slow cooker. Combine sugar and next 3 ingredients; sprinkle over roast. Combine broth and remaining ingredients, stirring well. Pour broth mixture over roast. (Do not stir.)
2. Cover and cook on HIGH 1 hour; reduce heat to LOW, and cook 8 hours or until roast is tender. Transfer roast to a cutting board; cut into large chunks, if desired. **Makes 8 to 10 servings.** **Note:** We tested with a dark lager beer.

Wild Horse Mountain BBQ

Sallisaw, Oklahoma

GPS COORDINATES:
Lat./Long. 35.46051,-94.790318

Highway 59 74955
(918) 775-9960

Don't Miss:

Green Sign

The plain green sign at the top of the mountain that says "Wild Horse BBQ Road" is easy to miss, so keep your eyes peeled. Also, be careful with the sauces. As they say here, "Hot is real hot. Medium is kinda hot. Mild is baby sauce."

You're going to cuss me if you try to find this remote shack in the woods without a GPS or a sherpa of some kind. Signage is minimal. So is the menu. Decorations are "mantiques," such as a pocket knife collection. But all that fades as you bite into one of Wild Horse's ribs (and no, they're not from a horse). The restaurant's killer barbecue sauce, baked beans, and dry-rubbed ribs will keep you coming back—and trust me, next time you'll remember how to find it.

Dry Rub

- 3   Tbsp. coarse sea salt
- 3   Tbsp. dry mustard
- 3   Tbsp. pepper
- 3   Tbsp. Worcestershire powder

1. Stir together all ingredients. Store in an airtight container. **Makes ¾ cup.**

Note: Order the Worcestershire powder online if your store doesn't carry it.

* Diner Secret: Canned beans jump-start this easy recipe for a crowd.

* Diner Secret: Coat ribs in dry rub, and cook them long and slow so meat is flavorful fall-off-the-bone tender.

BBQ Beans

- 1½   cups barbecue sauce
- ½   cup firmly packed brown sugar
- 1   Tbsp. paprika
- 1   (53-oz.) can pork and beans
- ½   lb. pulled smoked pork, coarsely chopped

1. Preheat oven to 375°. Combine all ingredients in a large bowl, stirring well. Pour into an ungreased 13- x 9-inch baking dish. Bake, uncovered, at 375° for 25 minutes. **Makes 12 servings.**

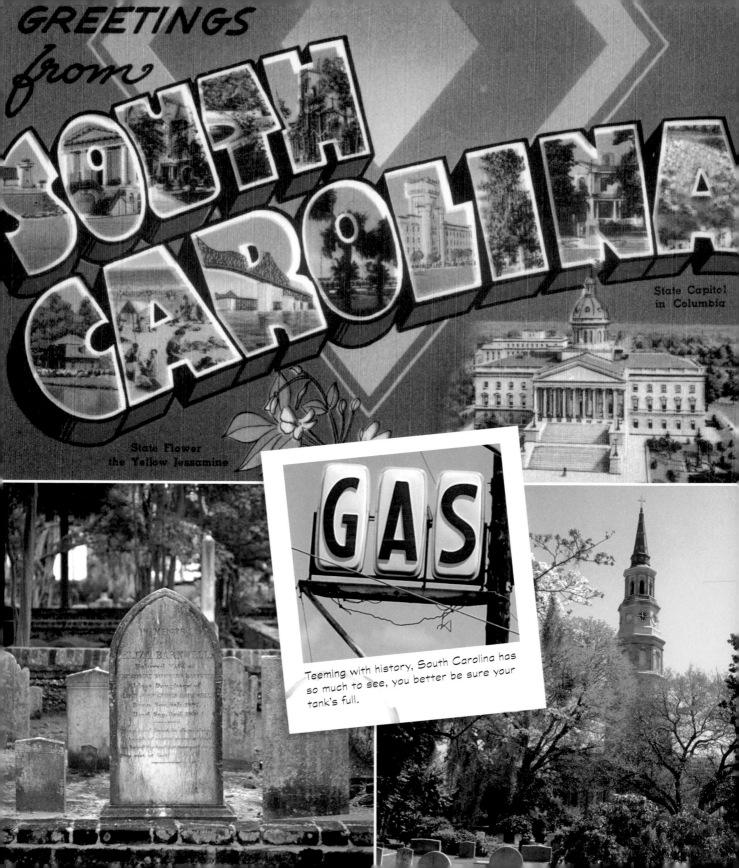

GREETINGS *from* SOUTH CAROLINA

State Capitol in Columbia

State Flower the Yellow Jessamine

GAS

Teeming with history, South Carolina has so much to see, you better be sure your tank's full.

South Carolina

Best Drive

Charleston to Savannah

T he drive between these two queen cities of the South is perhaps one of the most majestic and satisfying that you'll find in our region. I never visit this part of the country without taking this exact journey. It's full of historic rice plantations, nature preserves, lonely old gas stations, and wide country views. Stop off in quaint Beaufort if you're looking to break it up, or keep on trucking until you get a sniff of the pungent mud smell (the sweet smell of home to those of us who have loved ones in the lowcountry).

Length: 113 miles

South Carolina

185

Carolina Cider Co.

Yemassee, South Carolina

GPS COORDINATES:
Lat./Long. 32.604987, -80.755379

81 Charleston Highway 29945
(843) 846-1899
www.carolinaciderco.com

Don't Miss:

Passing Time

While every other traveler between Charleston and Savannah is zooming in and out of fast food joints and smelly rest stops, you can mosey into the Carolina Cider Co., order up some peanuts and Co-Colas, and then sit out on the rocking chairs. Bliss!

TODAY'S FRESH BAKED

PIES

Peach

Cherry

Pecan

APPLE

Blueberry

Sweet Potato

Pecan
Apple
Blueberry Cri
Cookies
hocolate Chi

Boiled peanuts are to the South what violent taxi rides are to New York City—you'll find them regularly across our region. Gas stations, shacks, and other itinerate outposts of Dixie may serve up a cup of flabby goobers, but to sample the best, stop at this old general store. Not only can you buy all the jams, syrups, relishes, preserves, and molasses your heart desires, but the grits, teas, and sweetgrass baskets make it a shopper's paradise.

Spicy Cajun Boiled Peanuts

The ingredients for this recipe can easily be halved to make a smaller batch.

- 2   lb. raw Virginia peanuts in shell
- ½   cup kosher salt
- ¼   cup crushed red pepper
- ¼   cup Cajun seasoning
- 2   Tbsp. hot sauce

1. Wash raw peanuts in shell. Soak peanuts in water to cover 45 minutes to loosen any remaining dirt. Drain peanuts, and rinse well under cold running water.

2. Place peanuts, salt, and remaining ingredients in a 12-qt. Dutch oven. Add 1¾ gal. water; stir well. Cover and bring to a boil; reduce heat, and simmer 4 to 6 hours or until tender. (Peanuts are done when texture is tender and firm, but not crunchy—similar to cooked pinto beans.)

3. Drain peanuts, and store in zip-top plastic bags in refrigerator up to 2 weeks, or freeze in zip-top plastic freezer bags up to 2 months. **Makes 18 cups.**

* Diner Secret: A splash of freshly squeezed lemon juice brightens the sweet berry flavor.

Blackberry Jam

Blackberry brambles are a chigger's favorite hideout. This jam is worth the blood-letting.

- 4   cups crushed blackberries (about 1½ qt. whole berries)
- 2   Tbsp. lemon juice
- 1   (1¾-oz.) package powdered pectin
- 6   cups sugar

1. Stir together first 3 ingredients in a Dutch oven.

2. Bring mixture to a full rolling boil. Add sugar, stirring constantly, and bring to a full rolling boil. Boil 1 minute. Remove from heat. Skim off any foam with a metal spoon.

3. Pour hot jam immediately into hot, sterilized jars, filling to ⅛ inch from top; wipe jar rims. Cover at once with metal lids, and screw on bands.

4. Process in boiling water bath 10 minutes. Remove jars from boiling water bath, and let stand at room temperature for 24 hours. **Makes about 6 half-pints.**

Grits and Groceries

Saylors Crossroads, South Carolina

GPS COORDINATES:
Lat./Long. 34.398913,-82.507008

2440 Due West Highway 29627
(864) 296-3316
www.gritsandgroceries.info

Don't Miss:

Heidi's Dinner

Grits and Groceries is normally just open for breakfast and lunch, but if you ask Heidi nicely, she might invite you to her monthly Saturday evening dinner. You'll eat what she serves and be expected to dance to the live music. It's a feast worth experiencing.

Southern cookin'
keeps ya good lookin'
www.gritsandgroceries.com

So you've never heard of Saylors Crossroads? It's 12 miles from Anderson, 9 miles from Belton, and due east from the town of Due West…oh, whatever. It's remote. But take this advice: Make the trip. Hire a guide if you have to. Owners Heidi and Joe Trull are culinary magicians, slavishly devoted to the finest ingredients, local farmers, and rich Southern tradition. They show off their knack for invention in dishes such as honeysuckle ice cream and tomato pie, which have now made Saylors Crossroads the center of my universe.

Tomato Pie

4 medium-size ripe tomatoes
2 tsp. salt
1 cup (4 oz.) shredded Cheddar cheese
1 cup mayonnaise
1 Tbsp. chopped fresh basil
1 Tbsp. chopped fresh parsley
¼ tsp. pepper
1 small onion, finely chopped
½ (14.1-oz.) package refrigerated piecrusts

1. Preheat oven to 350°. Slice tomatoes into ¼-inch-thick slices. Arrange tomato slices on several layers of paper towels over a wire rack. Sprinkle with 2 tsp. salt; cover with more paper towels, pressing gently. Let salted tomatoes stand 1 hour, replacing paper towels on top and bottom after 30 minutes.

2. Combine cheese, mayonnaise, herbs, pepper, and onion in a medium bowl; stir well, and set aside. Roll piecrust into a 13-inch circle on a flat surface. Fit into a 9-inch pie plate; fold edges under, and crimp. Firmly pat tomato slices dry with additional paper towels. Arrange tomato slices in piecrust; top with cheese mixture.

3. Bake at 350° on lowest oven rack for 40 minutes or until golden brown. Cool completely on a wire rack. **Makes 8 servings.**

✱ Diner Secret: Drain the tomatoes on paper towels to absorb maximum moisture before baking.

South Carolina

189

* Diner Secret: A signature seasoning blend makes this dish special.

South Carolina Shrimp Gravy and Grits

The generous amount of seasoning leaves enough left over to use in other seafood recipes.

10	bacon slices, chopped
1	cup chopped onion
1	cup chopped green bell pepper
1	cup chopped celery
2	Tbsp. all-purpose flour
1	Tbsp. Low Country Seasoning
2	Tbsp. Worcestershire sauce
2	tsp. finely chopped fresh thyme
2	lb. raw shrimp, peeled
1¼	cup (10-oz.) beef broth

Hot cooked grits
Garnish: fresh thyme

1. Cook bacon in a large skillet over medium-high heat until almost crisp. Add onion, bell pepper, and celery; cook, stirring often, 8 minutes or until vegetables are tender and bacon is crisp.

2. Stir in flour; cook, stirring constantly, 1 minute. Stir in Low Country Seasoning, Worcestershire sauce, and 2 tsp. thyme. Stir in shrimp. Cook, stirring constantly, 3 minutes. Stir in beef broth. Cook, stirring often, 4 minutes or just until shrimp turn pink and sauce is thickened. Serve over grits. Garnish, if desired. **Makes 7 servings.**

Low Country Seasoning

¼	cup celery salt
1	Tbsp. kosher salt
2	Tbsp. garlic powder
2	Tbsp. ground white pepper
2½	Tbsp. dry mustard
2	Tbsp. ground red pepper
1½	Tbsp. ground bay leaf
2	Tbsp. black pepper

1. Stir together all ingredients in a medium bowl until blended. Store in an airtight container. **Makes 1 cup.**

"Eat more shrimp-n-grits!"

Southern Fried Catfish

Creole Seasoning

2 Tbsp. kosher salt
2 Tbsp. garlic powder
2 Tbsp. paprika
1 Tbsp. onion powder
1½ Tbsp. pepper
1 Tbsp. ground red pepper
1 tsp. celery salt
1 tsp. dried oregano
1 tsp. dried thyme

Catfish

Vegetable oil
2 cups cornmeal
2 cups masa harina (corn flour)
2 large eggs
1 cup milk
1 Tbsp. Creole mustard
3 lb. farm-raised catfish fillets, cut into
    4- x 2-inch strips
Parchment paper
Pickled vegetables
Sliced tomatoes

1. **Prepare Creole Seasoning:** Combine all ingredients in a medium bowl, stirring well.
2. **Prepare Catfish:** Preheat oven to 300°. Pour oil to a depth of 3 inches into a 4- to 5-qt. Dutch oven; heat over medium-high heat to 350°.
3. Meanwhile, combine cornmeal, masa harina, and 3 Tbsp. Creole Seasoning in a large bowl, reserving remaining seasoning for another use. Stir seasoning mixture well.
4. Whisk eggs in a large bowl; whisk in milk and mustard. Dip fish in egg mixture; dredge in cornmeal mixture, shaking off excess.

This flaky fried catfish is laced with home-made Creole Seasoning for kick.

5. [text obscured]
sid[text obscured]
a b[text obscured]
in [text obscured]
Ser[text obscured]
toe[text obscured]

Magnolia Bakery

Beaufort, South Carolina

GPS COORDINATES:
Lat./Long. 32.438727,-80.669929

703 Congress Street 29902

(843) 524-1961

Don't Miss:

Pecan Pie

Which dessert to order? Go for the pecan pie. Tall, smooth, creamy, and sweet, it is a true Southern masterpiece.

It doesn't get more Southern than this café. The long main dining room is haphazardly stuffed with various decorative accessories, but it isn't so girly that a guy would feel odd ordering a rare roast beef sandwich. When you walk in, check out the display of desserts. Your glucose levels will spike just looking at them. For lunch, enjoy the lovely mixed-green salad perfectly topped with a sweet house-made poppy-seed dressing. An entire family of crabs must perish to create one delicious crabcake sandwich, seared to a golden brown and served with a tart pasta salad.

Pasta Salad

8	oz. tri-color rotini pasta
½	cup olive oil
2	Tbsp. red wine vinegar
1	Tbsp. chopped green onions
2	tsp. sugar
1	tsp. garlic powder
1	tsp. dried basil
1	tsp. Dijon mustard
½	tsp. salt
½	tsp. dried oregano
¼	tsp. freshly ground pepper
½	cup shredded carrots
2	(2.5-oz.) cans sliced black olives, drained

1. Cook pasta according to package directions; drain. Rinse under cold running water until cool. Drain well.
2. Stir together oil and next 9 ingredients in a large bowl. Add pasta, carrots, and olives; toss well. **Makes 6 servings.**

Butternut Squash Soup

Soup

1	medium leek
1	Tbsp. unsalted butter
1	medium onion, diced
1	large butternut squash (2 lb.), peeled and cubed
1	medium carrot, chopped
½	tsp. ground nutmeg
¼	tsp. ground cloves
¼	tsp. salt
¼	tsp. ground white pepper
2	cups chicken stock
1	cup whipping cream

Topping

1	cup crème fraîche
½	cup chopped pecans, toasted
2	Tbsp. bourbon
½	tsp. salt
½	tsp. minced fresh sage

1. **Prepare Soup:** Remove and discard root ends and dark green tops of leeks. Cut in half lengthwise, and rinse thoroughly under cold running water to remove grit and sand. Chop leek.
2. Melt butter in a Dutch oven over medium heat. Add leek and onion. Cook, stirring often, 12 minutes or until tender. Add squash and next 5 ingredients; cook, stirring often, 2 minutes. Stir in stock. Bring to a boil; cover, reduce heat, and simmer 25 minutes or until vegetables are tender.
3. **Meanwhile, prepare Topping:** Stir together all ingredients in a medium bowl.
4. Remove soup from heat; stir in cream. Process soup, in batches, in a blender until smooth. Dollop each serving with topping. **Makes 6 cups.**

Magnolia Bakery Café's Lemon Bars

Parchment paper

1	cup unsalted butter
2	cups all-purpose flour
½	cup powdered sugar
4	large eggs
2	cups granulated sugar
½	cup fresh lemon juice (about 4 lemons)
2	Tbsp. lemon zest
3	Tbsp. all-purpose flour
1	tsp. baking powder

Powdered sugar

1. Preheat oven to 350°. Line a lightly greased 13- x 9-inch pan with parchment paper. Place butter in a 4-cup glass measuring cup. Cover and microwave at HIGH 1 minute or until melted. Let cool 8 minutes.
2. Whisk together melted butter, 2 cups flour, and ½ cup powdered sugar in a bowl until blended. Press mixture onto bottom of prepared pan. Bake at 350° for 20 minutes or until lightly browned.
3. Meanwhile, whisk eggs in a medium bowl until blended. Whisk in granulated sugar and next 2 ingredients. Stir together 3 Tbsp. flour and baking powder; whisk into egg mixture. Pour filling evenly over hot baked crust.
4. Bake at 350° for 25 to 30 minutes or until filling is set. Let cool in pan on a wire rack 30 minutes. Lift from pan, using parchment as handles. Cool completely on a wire rack. Chill, if desired. Cut into bars, and dust generously with powdered sugar before serving. **Makes 2 dozen.**

Roz's Rice Mill Café

Pawleys Island, South Carolina

GPS COORDINATES:

Lat./Long. 33.439812,-79.126328

10880 Ocean Highway 29585

(843) 235-0196

www.rozsricemillcafe.com

Don't Miss:

*Black Bean–
Artichoke Cake*

Roz makes a black bean–artichoke cake served with tart salsa, sour cream, and fresh limes that will make you want to move to Pawleys Island so you can eat here every day.

✳ Diner Secret: Panko breadcrumbs lend a welcome crunch to these tender vegetarian cakes.

Soup? At the beach? If you're under the impression that beach food is all about tidal waves of fried fish, shrimp, and hush puppies, you need to come to Roz's tiny bistro. To start, it's cheap like the devil. You can eat a huge lunch for less than $10. Better still, that lunch will be unforgettable. Take the mushroom, sherry, and crab soup—an incredibly creamy, dense concoction made for people who like to eat their soups with a fork. One delicious cupful is a meal in and of itself; a bowl is a feast. Dig in and bliss out.

Black Bean–Artichoke Cakes

Artichokes are an unexpected addition to these hearty bean cakes that can be served as an entrée or made smaller and plated as an appetizer.

4	cups canned black beans, drained and rinsed
1	cup coarsely chopped canned artichoke hearts
2	Tbsp. ground cumin
1	Tbsp. chili powder
2	tsp. dried oregano
1	tsp. dried thyme
2	tsp. Dijon mustard
¼	tsp. salt
¼	tsp. pepper
3	cups Japanese breadcrumbs (panko), divided
¼	cup canola oil

Sour cream

Fresh salsa

1. Mash together first 9 ingredients in a large bowl, using a potato masher. Stir in 2 cups Japanese breadcrumbs. Shape bean mixture into 12 (3-inch) patties using about ⅓ to ½ cup for each patty.
2. Place remaining 1 cup breadcrumbs in a shallow plate. Dredge patties in breadcrumbs, pressing gently.
3. Heat 2 Tbsp. oil in a large nonstick skillet over medium-high heat. Fry half of patties in hot oil 2 minutes on each side; drain on a wire rack over paper towels. Repeat procedure with remaining 2 Tbsp. oil and patties. Serve with sour cream and salsa. **Makes 6 servings.**

Fulton Five

Charleston, South Carolina

For the best meals, eat where the locals go. Fulton Five has served up northern Italian food for the past 18 years. Begin with the warm spicy bresaola and a salad of spinach and thinly shaved dried beets. Warm, flattering light calls for hushed romantic conversations and big glasses of vino. The menu changes seasonally, but be sure to order a luscious dish to go with it all. I sampled the tonno alla griglia, a generous cut of caper-encrusted bluefin atop a creamy bed of sweet pea risotto. For dessert, try the dense, slightly crunchy pistachio ice cream. Its near-gelato texture is the perfect Italian finish. Take a peek at the mouthwatering dinner and dessert menus at www.fultonfive.net.

Food Find:

South Carolina

* Diner Secret: For added flavor, look for bakery focaccia with fresh tomatoes baked inside.

Portobello Mushrooms and Grilled Shrimp on Focaccia with Goat Cheese Spread

2 Tbsp. olive oil, divided
2 tsp. hoisin sauce
2 tsp. soy sauce
3 garlic cloves, divided
12 large raw shrimp, peeled and deveined
¼ cup (1 oz.) crumbled goat cheese, softened
2 Tbsp. sour cream
¼ tsp. salt
¼ tsp. freshly ground pepper
2 (4-inch) portobello caps
¼ tsp. garlic salt
1 (12-oz.) herbed focaccia loaf, split and toasted
2 cups fresh baby spinach

1. Preheat grill to 350° to 400° (medium-high) heat. Combine 1 Tbsp. oil, hoisin sauce, soy sauce, and 2 garlic cloves, minced, in a medium bowl. Add shrimp, tossing to coat. Cover and chill 30 minutes. Remove shrimp from marinade, discarding marinade.

2. Meanwhile, mince remaining garlic clove. Stir together minced garlic, goat cheese, and next 3 ingredients. Set aside.

3. Brush remaining Tbsp. oil on tops of portobello caps; sprinkle with garlic salt. Grill caps, covered with grill lid, 4 minutes on each side or until tender; cut into thin slices. Grill shrimp 2 minutes on each side or until done.

4. Spread reserved goat cheese mixture on cut sides of focaccia. Top bottom half of focaccia with mushroom caps, shrimp, spinach, and bread top. Cut sandwich into 4 wedges. **Makes 4 servings.**

Rubbernecker Wonder:
Dillon, South Carolina
SOB

Hundreds choose South of the Border (or "SOB" to those in the know) as the spot to tie the knot. Yes, scores of couples get married here every month, which would be alarming were the main attraction simply Pedro, the largest sign east of the Mississippi. But after all, SOB has souvenirs galore, a "Casateria," "Pedro's Pleasure Dome" (which, *si si*, contains the wedding chapel), and 135 acres of assorted roadside stuff. One visit to this quirky sombrero world just off I-95 and you'll be a convert…or at least supplied with a quality back scratcher.

Look!

Wade's Family Diner

Spartanburg, South Carolina

Lat./Long. 34.969187,-81.932856

1000 North Pine Street 29303

(864) 582-3800

www.eatatwades.com

Don't Miss:

Pie

The pie. Any pie. Our favorites? The fluffy peanut butter pie and the banana split pie. They are the perfect reward for having eaten all your vegetables.

Vegetables frolic on every wall of Wade's, highlighting their central status in this restaurant's menu. For Wade's is, truly, a Southern house of vegetables, and generations have enjoyed the classic fare served here. They boil a green bean like your mama, and her mama (read: no crunch allowed). It's the kind of place where waitresses still call you "sweetheart" and the yeast rolls are a meal unto themselves.

Banana Split Pie

1 cup powdered sugar
½ cup butter, softened
¼ cup egg substitute
½ tsp. vanilla extract
1 (6-oz.) ready-made graham cracker piecrust
2 bananas, sliced
1 (20-oz.) can crushed pineapple, drained
2 cups frozen whipped topping, thawed
Chopped pecans
Garnish: maraschino cherries with stems, chocolate
    sauce

1. Beat first 4 ingredients at medium speed with an electric mixer until smooth; spread in piecrust. Top filling with banana slices, pineapple, and whipped topping, sealing topping to edges. Sprinkle topping with pecans. Cover and chill at least 1 hour.
2. Garnish just before serving, if desired. **Makes 8 servings.**

Creamed Potatoes

5 lb. white potatoes, peeled and cut into
    1-inch pieces
3½ tsp. salt, divided
2 cups milk
¼ cup butter

1. Bring potatoes, 4 qt. water, and 1½ tsp. salt to a boil in a 6-qt. Dutch oven. Reduce heat, and simmer, uncovered, 18 minutes or until potatoes are tender. Drain.
2. Place milk in a 2-cup glass measuring cup. Microwave at HIGH 1 minute or until warm. Place butter in a large bowl; add potatoes. Add hot milk and remaining 2 tsp. salt. Beat at low speed with an electric mixer until blended; beat at medium speed 3 minutes or until fluffy. **Makes 10 to 12 servings.**

* Diner Secret: Heating the milk ensures that the potatoes will stay hot while being whipped.

"Hi Ho Hi Ho, Its Off To Work We Go"

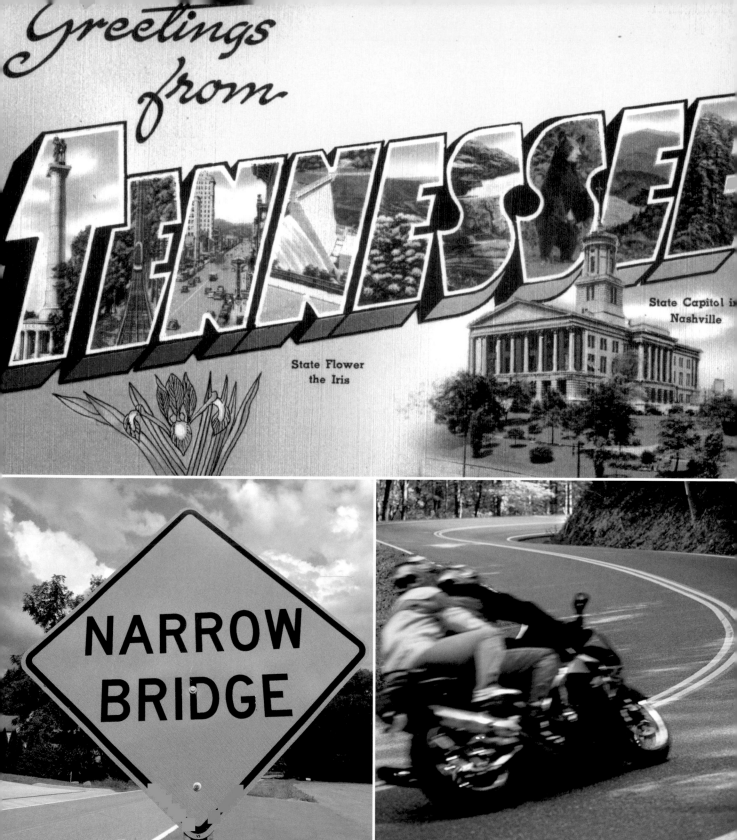

Tennessee

Best Drive

Tail of the Dragon

I found this section of Highway 129 by accident, trying to get from one restaurant to another in researching this book. Here are some tips: Don't think of this as a shortcut. Don't go on a full stomach. Don't go in a giant Cadillac. Don't take interns who get carsick. The Dragon is 11 miles long, but it covers just 6 miles as the crow flies. That means you're doubling back, and going up and down more than you'll believe possible. Originally a buffalo track, it is now prized by motorcycle riders and sports car owners, even though the speed limit is a mere 30 mph. **Length:** 11 miles

Benton's Smoky Mountain Country Hams

Madisonville, Tennessee

GPS COORDINATES:
Lat./Long. 35.56183,-84.297399

2603 U.S. 411 37354

(423) 442-5003

www.bentonscountryhams2.com

Don't Miss:
Prosciutto

Allan Benton's ham and sausage will delight, but his prosciutto would make even the most skeptical Italian cry *molto bene*! Yes, it can all be ordered by mail.

Ahhh, the hickory-smoked twang of bacon. I love it on a BLT, in a salad, or simply by itself. I've even had a romance start over a plate of good bacon (gotta love a woman who eats bacon with gusto). And the best bacon on the planet is made by Allan Benton. Its aged, smoky richness will cook up to just the right mixture of crispy and chewy. Allan's philosophy hasn't changed despite his growing fame: Buy the finest free-roaming hogs, cure them with salt and brown sugar, and smoke with hickory and applewood.

Benton's Bacon-Infused Cocktail

The idea of a bacon-bourbon cocktail was born at a bar named PDT in—of all places—New York City. Here's Mr. Benton's version.

2   Tbsp. bacon drippings
1   (750-ml.) bottle bourbon
Maple syrup
1   (4-oz.) bottle bitters
Garnish: orange zest twists

1. Strain bacon drippings into bourbon in a carafe or other pitcher. Let stand 8 hours.
2. Chill the bacon-infused bourbon until fat rises to the top; skim fat.
3. For each cocktail, pour ¼ cup bacon-infused bourbon into an old-fashioned glass filled with desired amount of ice; stir in 1 Tbsp. maple syrup and ⅛ tsp. bitters. Garnish, if desired. **Makes 16 servings.**

"We're a hillbilly operation through and through," says Allan Benton.

I asked Mr. Benton how to cook bacon. While this may sound like asking "How do you boil water?" the truth is, most people cook lousy bacon. When too burned or too flabby, bacon loses its magical properties. So, here's the secret:

Perfectly-cooked Bacon

1. Arrange thick-sliced bacon in a single layer in a well-seasoned, large cast-iron skillet. Cook over medium heat, flattening, poking, and turning bacon as it cooks. Cook 20 to 25 minutes or until crisp and the white of the bacon begins to tan. Remove bacon, and drain on paper towels. **Makes 5 slices per 12-inch cast-iron skillet.**
Note: Order Benton's thick, smoky bacon online; it's worth every penny.

Cooking perfect bacon is an artform. It shouldn't be too floppy or too crisp.

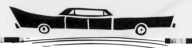

Cabana

Nashville, Tennessee

GPS COORDINATES:
Lat./Long. 36.137065,-86.799215

1910 Belcourt Avenue 37212
(615) 577-2262
www.cabananashville.com

Don't Miss:

Lobster Mac

I don't usually order seafood in a landlocked state but Cabana's lobster mac breaks that rule. The creamy, dense concoction will leave you feeling like you just left Maine…or heaven!

＊ Diner Secret: A sprinkling of confectioners' sugar is powder on the pie.

The understated elegance of Cabana may be why Nashville's celebrities flock here to sample the fantastic fare. Not long ago, I missed singers Taylor Swift and Jessie James (were I a teenage girl, I'd be squealing just writing their names). Why the star power? First off, you can order a fried pie and still feel chic. Really. Their trio of fried pies is my favorite dish in Tennessee. Also, the restaurant sits just blocks from Vanderbilt University, and the front and back bar are usually full of pretty people ordering pretty food.

Chocolate Fried Pies

Filling

1	cup sugar
½	cup all-purpose flour
½	cup unsweetened cocoa
⅛	tsp. salt
1	cup milk
¼	cup butter
2	tsp. vanilla extract

Fried Pie Dough

3	cups all-purpose flour
½	tsp. salt
½	cup plus 2 Tbsp. shortening, chilled
6	to 7 Tbsp. ice water
	Vegetable oil
1	large egg, lightly beaten
	Powdered sugar

1. **Prepare Filling:** Whisk together first 4 ingredients in a 3-qt. saucepan. Gradually whisk in milk. Cook, whisking constantly, over medium heat 9 minutes or until very thick. Reduce heat to low; stir in butter and vanilla. Remove from heat; cover and let cool to room temperature.

2. **Prepare Fried Pie Dough:** Place first 2 ingredients in a food processor, and pulse 3 or 4 times or until combined.

3. Add shortening, and pulse 5 or 6 times or until crumbly. Sprinkle ice water over flour mixture; pulse until flour mixture is moistened. Transfer from processor bowl to a floured surface, shaping into 2 balls.

4. Pour oil to depth of 1 inch in a Dutch oven; heat to 360°.

5. Meanwhile, roll out each ball of dough to ⅛-inch thickness; cut each into 3 (6-inch) circles. Spoon ⅓ cup filling into center of each circle. Brush edges of circles with egg; fold dough over filling, and crimp edges with a fork to seal.

6. Fry pies, 2 at a time, in hot oil 3 minutes or until golden. (Do not turn.) Drain pies on a rack over paper towels. Let cool completely. Sprinkle with powdered sugar just before serving. **Makes 6 servings.**

* Diner Secret: Lobster and Brie make this mac and cheese dinner party worthy.

Lobster & Brie Mac and Cheese

Luxurious comfort food at its finest.

1   tsp. olive oil
4   oz. thinly sliced prosciutto
10   oz. uncooked ditalini pasta
2   cups heavy cream
½   tsp. salt
½   tsp. pepper
5   oz. Brie cheese, cubed
¼   cup (1 oz.) freshly grated Parmesan cheese
2   cups chopped cooked lobster
2   Tbsp. chopped fresh chives
Garnish: 4 lobster claws

1. Heat olive oil in a large skillet over medium heat. Fry prosciutto in hot oil 2½ minutes on each side or until crisp; drain on paper towels. Crumble prosciutto.

2. Cook pasta in boiling salted water according to package directions. Drain.

3. Meanwhile, bring cream, salt, and pepper to a boil in a large skillet; reduce heat, and simmer, uncovered, 5 minutes or until reduced to 1⅓ cups. Stir in cheeses and pasta; cook 3 minutes or until cheeses melt and mixture is thickened. Stir in lobster; cook 3 minutes or until thoroughly heated.

4. To serve, spoon pasta onto 4 serving plates. Sprinkle with prosciutto and chives. Garnish each serving with a lobster claw, if desired.

Makes 4 servings.

The Flying Fish

Memphis, Tennessee

If you've had your fill of Memphis's famous 'cue, then head over to The Flying Fish for freshly-shucked oysters on the half shell served with sinus-clearing red sauce and delicate fried catfish at a bargain price. Less than $5 gets you a fried catfish fillet, French fries and a hush puppy. That's a fair price for stick-to-your-ribs goodness sans barbecue sauce. Whether you like your fish grilled, steamed, or boiled, Flying Fish serves it up your way seven days a week until 10 p.m. so you can refuel after taking in the sights and sounds on Beale Street. Go to www.flyingfishinthe.net to preview the entire menu.

Food Find:

Loveless Cafe and Motel

Nashville, Tennessee

GPS COORDINATES:

Lat./Long. 36.03581, -86.972158

8400 Highway 100 37221

(615) 646-9700

www.lovelesscafe.com

Don't Miss: *Hash Browns*

You may think hash browns just belong on a breakfast plate. Loveless will change that narrow mindset. Their hash brown casserole will slap that simple side into a whole new reality. Hash browns with fried chicken! Hash browns with ham! I could go on!

Perfect sweet tea. Crispy fried chicken. Heavenly hashbrown casserole. Oh, and then there's the biscuits. When Carol Fay, head biscuit maker at this Nashville institution, passed away in 2010, it made front-page news and was reported around the world. Why? Because the biscuits are that good. You'll want to get here early, as weekend wait times can be as much as two hours. Don't worry: Boutique shops, art galleries, and even a bike store will keep you entertained while you wait for that pile of biscuits.

Hash Brown Casserole

2   cups chopped onions
2   (20-oz.) packages refrigerated shredded
     hash browns
2   (8-oz.) packages shredded Cheddar cheese
2   (10¾-oz.) cans cream of chicken soup
1   (16-oz.) container sour cream
2   tsp. salt
1   tsp. pepper

1. Preheat oven to 350°. Stir together onions, hash browns, and cheese in a very large bowl. Whisk together soup and remaining ingredients in another bowl until blended. Pour over potato mixture, stirring to coat.
2. Spoon potato mixture into a greased 13- x 9-inch baking dish. Bake, uncovered, at 350° for 1 hour and 15 minutes or until browned. **Makes 12 servings.**
Note: Substitute shredded Italian cheese for one of the packages of shredded Cheddar for depth.

Pecan Pie

½   (14.1-oz.) package refrigerated piecrusts
1½   cups pecan halves
3   large eggs
1   cup light corn syrup
½   cup firmly packed brown sugar
¼   cup unsalted butter, melted
1   tsp. vanilla extract
¼   tsp. ground cinnamon

1. Preheat oven to 350°. Fit piecrust into a 9-inch pie plate according to package directions; fold edges under, and crimp. Place pecan halves in bottom of piecrust.
2. Whisk eggs in a medium bowl; whisk in remaining ingredients until blended. Pour filling over pecan halves.
3. Bake at 350° for 1 hour. Let cool completely on a wire rack. **Makes 8 servings.**

George Harvell's Watermelon Ribs

These ultra-tender ribs are on the salty side. If desired, cut back on the dry rub. St. Louis–style ribs are spareribs with the top bony and fatty section trimmed off, leaving single vertical bones.

6   cups hickory wood chunks
2   racks St. Louis–style pork spareribs (8½ lb.)
1   (4.5-oz) jar dry barbecue rub (¾ cup)
½   cup firmly packed dark brown sugar
1   (18-oz.) bottle barbecue sauce
½   cup small watermelon cubes

1. Soak hickory chunks in water to cover at least 1 hour; drain. Place 3 cups wood chunks in center of each of 2 large squares of heavy-duty aluminum foil; fold each into a rectangle, and seal. Punch holes in tops of packets.

2. Light one side of grill, heating to 250° to 300° (low) heat; leave other side unlit. Place 1 packet on cooking grate over lit side.

3. Meanwhile, remove thin membrane from back of ribs by slicing into it with a knife and then pulling it off. Combine dry rub and brown sugar; rub mixture over both sides of rib racks. Place ribs, bone side down, over unlit side, and smoke, covered with grill lid, 2 hours. Add remaining packet of hickory chunks to lit side of grill. Turn ribs over; cover and smoke 2 more hours.

4. Preheat oven to 300°. Cut ribs, slicing between every 3 bones; place in a large roasting pan. Pour barbecue sauce over ribs. Sprinkle with water-melon cubes; tightly cover pan with aluminum foil. Bake at 300° for 2 hours or until ribs are tender. (Meat should separate easily from bone.) **Makes 8 servings.**

* Diner Secret: The watermelon, of course!

* Diner Secret: Petite-diced tomatoes save time prepping tomatoes for this hearty meatloaf.

Carol Fay's Famous Meatloaf

½   cup chopped onion
1   Tbsp. chopped garlic
2   tsp. vegetable oil
1   large egg
⅓   cup steak sauce
2   tsp. garlic powder
2   tsp. seasoned salt
1   tsp. pepper
2   lb. ground round
¾   cup drained petite diced tomatoes
⅓   cup uncooked quick-cooking oats
½   cup barbecue sauce

1. Preheat oven to 350°. Sauté onion and garlic in hot oil in a small skillet over medium heat 5 minutes or until tender. Whisk together egg and next 4 ingredients in a large bowl. Add ground beef and next 2 ingredients; combine, using hands. Shape mixture into a 9- x 5-inch loaf; place on a lightly greased rack in an aluminum foil–lined broiler pan.
2. Bake at 350° for 1 hour and 5 minutes or until no longer pink in center. Place barbecue sauce in a small bowl. Cover and microwave at HIGH 30 seconds or until warm. Spread barbecue sauce evenly on top of meatloaf. Let stand 10 minutes before serving. **Makes 8 servings.**

Rubbernecker Wonder:
Chattanooga, Tennessee
Quirky Museum

If you drive your car into a ditch in Chattanooga, you'll be pleased to know that the wrecker was invented in this fair metropolis. While you wait for your ride to be repaired, swing by this quirky museum. You might not think of a tow truck as being beautiful, but then you haven't seen one from the 1920s, now have you? Used to be that grand luxury cars were converted into wreckers because they were big, heavy, reliable machines. So swing by and admire the glittering tow trucks, J-hooks, and yes, famous wrecks, on display.

Look!

Southern Hands Family Dining

Collierville, Tennessee

GPS COORDINATES:

Lat./Long. 35.031151,-89.66835

150 U.S. Highway 72 East 38017

(901) 853-6758

www.southernhandsfamilydining.com

Hush Puppies

"About the only thing my momma could make better than me was cornbread, so one night I prayed for a great recipe. And would you believe, I dreamt how to make it?" says owner Betty Baskin. She baked her heaven-sent recipe in a mini-loaf pan from Wal-Mart. When Betty's mother tasted it, she just had three words to say: "You got me." The corn-bread loaves are now the most popular menu item at Southern Hands.

Cooking breakfast for your 10 brothers and sisters on a cotton farm in Mississippi will teach you how to make a meal that sticks to your ribs. "I'd make big meals for breakfast like fried chicken and cornbread," twinkles Southern Hands' owner Betty Baskin. Today that's exactly what you'll get at her Memphis restaurants: turnip greens, candied yams, pork chops, fried chicken, boiled okra, baked spaghetti, and fried catfish. Betty's welcoming smile and heavenly cooking attract everyone from firefighters to head ministers to her family house of fine eating.

* Diner Secret: 1 Tbsp. water makes just the right amount of moisture to deliciously glaze these yams.

Candied Yams

6 lb. sweet potatoes, peeled and cut into ¼-inch slices
3 cups sugar
½ cup unsalted butter, cut into pieces
3 Tbsp. vanilla extract
2 Tbsp. ground cinnamon

1. Place 1 Tbsp. water and all ingredients in a 6-qt. Dutch oven. Bring to a boil over high heat; cover, reduce heat, and simmer 25 minutes or until potatoes are tender and glazed, stirring occasionally. **Makes 12 servings.**

Cornbread

2⅓ cups self-rising cornmeal
⅓ cup sugar
4 large eggs
1 cup vegetable oil
½ cup buttermilk
¼ cup unsalted butter, melted

1. Preheat oven to 425°. Combine cornmeal and sugar in a large bowl; make a well in center of mixture.
2. Whisk together eggs and next 3 ingredients; add to dry mixture, whisking until blended. Spoon into a greased (12-cup) muffin pan, filling two-thirds full.
3. Bake at 425° for 15 minutes until golden. Serve warm. **Makes 1 dozen.**

* Diner Secret: Unlike traditional cornbread, this batter must be whipped well to incorporate the oil and butter.

GREETINGS from TEXAS

State Capital in Austin

Longhorns with great breeding can fetch close to $50k. And that's no bull!

Texas

Best Drive

Bluebonnet Trails

When it's springtime in the Lone Star State, the Hill Country blooms to life with the most celebrated flower in Texas: bluebonnets. Named for the bonnet shape of their petals, they grow wild here and bloom from mid March to approximately May. Not planning a spring visit? No worries. Follow the Texas Wine Trail (www.texaswinetrail.com), and flowers or no, you'll have a great time in the Hill Country. Towns such as Fredericksburg, Kerrville, Marble Falls, and Dripping Springs will enchant visitors in search of true local flavor. **Length:** varies

Texas

215

Goode Co. Seafood

Houston, Texas

GPS COORDINATES:
Lat./Long. 29.728296,-95.420229

2621 Westpark Drive 77098

(713) 523-7154

www.goodecompany.com

Don't Miss:

Ceviche

Though its origins are more South American than Mexican, Goode Co.'s ceviche is one of the best I've tried. And talk about healthy! Fresh lime juice, seafood, and onion are tossed together and "cooked" by the acidity of the citrus.

The old stainless-steel Amtrak dining car, now permanently lodged in shrubbery, sports one of the coolest restaurants in Texas. Battered green stools, neon lights, and tile floors complete the look. I've never been disappointed by any dish on the menu, but what keeps me coming back is one dish in particular—Campechana De Mariscos (shrimp-and-crab Mexican seafood cocktails). Served in a sundae glass with a side of fresh chips, this tangy appetizer has an almost creamy quality that complements the bite of its fresh lime juice. Huge chunks of crab and shrimp make these ceviches well worth the splurge.

Campechana De Mariscos

Our testers gave this Mexican seafood cocktail our highest rating.

- 1   cup tomato-clam juice cocktail
- ½   cup ketchup
- ½   cup chili sauce
- ⅓   cup extra virgin olive oil
- ¼   cup fresh lime juice (about 2 limes)
- ¼   cup chopped fresh parsley
- ¼   cup pimiento-stuffed Spanish olives, chopped
- 1   Tbsp. chopped fresh oregano
- 1   tsp. minced garlic
- 1   serrano pepper, seeded and chopped
- ½   tsp. salt
- 1   (4-oz.) can chopped green chiles, drained
- ½   cup diced seeded tomato
- ¼   cup diced white onion
- ¼   cup chopped fresh cilantro
- ½   lb. unpeeled, medium-size raw shrimp (31/40 count), cooked and peeled
- ½   lb. fresh lump crabmeat, drained
- 1   avocado, peeled and diced

Thin tortilla chips

Garnishes: finely chopped seeded jalapeños

1. Stir together first 12 ingredients in a large bowl. Add tomato and next 4 ingredients, stirring gently. Add avocado; toss gently.

2. Spoon seafood mixture into ice-cream sundae glasses. Serve with tortilla chips. Garnish, if desired. **Makes 8 to 10 servings.**

Note: We tested with Clamato Tomato Clam Cocktail.

Take home Mexican candies such as fruity "tamarindo" and canlea-spiked chocolates.

H&H Carwash and Coffee Shop

El Paso, Texas

Lat./Long. 31.766287, -106.486712

701 East Yandell Drive 79902
(915) 533-1144

Don't Miss:

All the Machines

I've driven more than 25,000 miles in my vintage car in the past year. My secret to keeping it clean? All-cotton towels and a spray bottle of water. Though I must admit it's nice to let H&H Carwash do the work while I simply clean my plate.

Last time I drove my vintage car across Texas I ended up with dust, grit, and tumbleweeds all over my old blue beauty. Nothing hobbles your get-along like a dirty Cadillac, so I wheeled into H&H Carwash and Coffee Shop. I could live here, as it combines coffee, a car wash, and some of the best chow in town. Outside, old guys towel your car down. Inside, the chiles rellenos are a cheese-laden triumph with a delicate crust batter. The sweet chiles have a deep smoky flavor, and the whole affair maintains a crunch despite all the thick cheese. Tortillas come in a never-ending wave of warm corn and flour.

Chiles Rellenos

Monterey Jack or another cheese that melts well may be used.

Sauce

½ cup canned tomato sauce

½ tsp. garlic powder

¼ tsp. salt

Dash of pepper

1 medium-size green bell pepper, chopped

1 medium onion, chopped

3 small tomatoes, chopped

Chiles Rellenos

12 Anaheim peppers

1 lb. Muenster cheese, cut into 12 (3½- x ¾-inch) sticks

Vegetable oil

6 egg whites

4 egg yolks

1 cup all-purpose flour

✳ Diner Secret: Don't rinse the skins of the peppers or you'll lose their smoky, fire-roasted flavor.

1. **Prepare Sauce:** Combine all ingredients in a 4-qt. Dutch oven. Bring to a boil over medium-high heat; boil, uncovered, 7 minutes or until vegetables are tender. Remove from heat, and set aside.

2. **Prepare Chiles Rellenos:** Preheat grill to 400° to 450° (medium-high) heat. Place peppers on grill grate, and grill, covered with grill lid, 6 minutes on each side or until charred. Place peppers in a large zip-top plastic freezer bag. Seal bag; let stand 10 minutes to loosen skins. Peel peppers.

3. Cut a small lengthwise slit at the top of each pepper, leaving stems intact; remove and discard seeds. Carefully stuff 1 cheese stick into each pepper, overlap sides of slit to cover cheese.

4. Pour oil to depth of ½ inch in a large cast-iron skillet; heat to 360°.

5. Meanwhile, whisk egg whites until foamy. Place egg yolks in a separate bowl; whisk until blended. Whisk yolks into whites until fluffy.

6. Place flour in a shallow dish. Dredge each of 3 peppers in flour; dip in egg. Fry coated peppers in hot oil 3 minutes on each side or until golden brown. Drain peppers on paper towels. Repeat procedure 3 times with remaining peppers, egg, and flour, skimming fried cheese particles from oil between batches.

7. Spoon ½ cup sauce onto each of 6 serving plates. Nestle 2 Chiles Rellenos in sauce on each plate. **Makes 6 servings.**

H&H Coffee Shop Burritos

Serve these mild-flavored burritos with all the trimmings—chopped cilantro, a side of salsa, a dollop of sour cream, and a squeeze of lime.

2   Tbsp. canola oil
1   cup diced onion
1   (1-lb.) tri-tip beef steak*
2   jalapeño peppers, diced
5   plum tomatoes, diced
2   garlic cloves, minced
1   beef bouillon cube, crushed
Salt and pepper to taste
6   (10-inch) burrito-size flour tortillas, warmed

1. Heat oil in a large skillet over medium heat. Add onion; sauté 5 minutes or until tender.

2. Meanwhile, trim beef, and cut into ½-inch pieces. Add beef and jalapeños to skillet. Increase heat to high, and cook 4 minutes. Add tomatoes, garlic, and crushed bouillon; stir well. Cover and simmer over low heat 30 minutes or until beef is tender. Season with salt and pepper to taste.

3. Using a slotted spoon, spoon beef mixture evenly down center of each tortilla; roll up.

Makes 3 servings.

Note: We did not seed jalapeño peppers. For an even milder entrée, seed peppers before chopping.

*The tri-tip is a full-flavor, lean, low-cost steak cut from the tri-tip roast. Top sirloin may be substituted.

Rubbernecker Wonder:
Amarillo, Texas
Crop of Cadillacs

Like some bizarre crop of Detroit iron, 10 vintage Cadillacs lay buried in a field just 8 miles outside of Amarillo. Their exposed ends lure thousands of visitors, many of whom seem compelled to decorate these finned behemoths. Graffiti covers each car in more than an inch of paint, which probably has saved these beasts from rusting into one great oxidized heap.

These finned Caddisaurs that once roamed the roads now lure tourists and paint.

Highland Park Pharmacy

Dallas, Texas

Lat./Long. 32.823532,-96.7899

3229 Knox Street 75205

(214) 521-2126

Limeades

Limeades are a soda-fountain classic you won't want to miss. Tart, sweet, and icy, Highland Park Pharmacy's version has been a refreshing institution since 1912.

A food processor makes this 3-ingredient sandwich filling a snap to prepare.

Tooling around Dallas' posh Highland Park neighborhood, you might not imagine that there's any place affordable to grab a bite. Not so, fellow traveller. Point your car towards this venerable classic, lodged in a tiny Art Nouveaux building. Once a pharmacy, as the name suggests, it now dishes out soda-fountain classics, sandwiches, and sweets. While many a lunch counter has disappeared across the country, this one is still serving up delicious grilled pimiento cheese sandwiches and ham salad.

Ham Salad

1½ lb. cooked ham, cut into 1-inch cubes
1   cup mayonnaise
2   hard-cooked eggs, peeled and quartered

1. Process ham cubes in a food processor until coarsely chopped. Add mayonnaise and eggs. Pulse until finely chopped. Transfer ham salad to a bowl. Cover and chill until ready to serve. **Makes 12 to 15 servings.**

Pimiento Cheese

Doesn't get any simpler than this.

1¼ lb. mild Cheddar cheese, finely shredded
1   cup mayonnaise
2   (4-oz.) jars diced pimiento, drained

1. Stir together all ingredients until blended. Cover and chill until ready to serve. **Makes 15 servings.**

La Fogata

San Antonio, Texas

Lat./Long. 29.495863,-98.535265

2427 Vance Jackson Road 78213

(210) 340-1337

www.lafogata.com

Don't Miss:

Margaritas

Order one (or more) of La Fogata's fabulous margaritas, which comes garnished with stunning orchid blooms. It's one of the best you'll find in the area.

Texas brims with fantastic Mexican restaurants of every flavor and variety. But if you're looking for simple, authentic, and delicious fare, stop here on your way back to the airport. The lush oasis of chirping birds, trickling fountains, and extravagant plantings seem wildly out of place in this rather battered neighborhood. No matter. As soon as you're inside you'll want to get down to business with their dark and smoky salsa, tender pork tacos, and sticky-sweet tres leches cake.

Cochinita Pibil

Look for dried cascabel and ancho chiles in a Mexican supermarket.

½ cup olive oil
2 ancho chiles
2 dried cascabel chiles, stems removed
2 cups fresh orange juice
¼ cup chopped yellow onion
¼ cup white vinegar
2 tsp. jarred chicken soup base
1 tsp. minced fresh garlic
½ tsp. salt
3 oz. achiote paste
1½ lb. boneless pork loin roast
Hot cooked rice
Chopped red onion

1. Heat oil in a 10-inch skillet over medium-high heat. Remove stems from chiles. Cook chiles in hot oil 3 minutes or until softened, turning often. Process chiles, oil, orange juice, and next 6 ingredients in a blender until smooth.
2. Place pork in a large zip-top plastic freezer bag; pour chile mixture over meat. Seal bag, and marinate in refrigerator 20 minutes.
3. Preheat oven to 300°. Remove pork from marinade, reserving marinade. Place pork in a small roasting pan; pour marinade over pork. Bake, uncovered, at 300° for 2 hours and 30 minutes or until a meat thermometer inserted in thickest portion registers 155°, basting occasionally. Cover and let stand 10 to 12 minutes or until thermometer registers 160°.
4. Remove pork from pan; pour sauce into a bowl. Cut pork into ½-inch cubes; stir into sauce. Spoon rice into shallow bowls. Spoon pork mixture over rice; sprinkle with red onion. **Makes 4 to 6 servings.**

✱ Diner Secret: Achiote paste, made from annatto seed, gives this pork dish its rich russet hue.

Piñatas and chili pepper ristras set a lively Latin tone.

Enchiladas Verdes

1½ lb. fresh tomatillos, husks removed
4 serrano peppers
½ cup chopped onion
1 tsp. garlic powder
2 tsp. jarred chicken soup base
2 tsp. sugar
½ tsp. ground cumin
¼ cup olive oil
2 tsp. all-purpose flour
8 (6-inch) fajita-size corn tortillas
4 cups shredded cooked chicken
1½ cups (6 oz.) crumbled queso fresco (fresh
    Mexican cheese)
Garnish: diced red onions

1. Preheat broiler with oven rack 5½ inches from heat. Place tomatillos and peppers on a rimmed baking sheet. Broil 15 minutes or until blistered, turning once. Remove pepper stems.

2. Preheat oven to 400°. Process tomatillos, peppers, ½ cup onion, and next 4 ingredients in a blender until pureed.

3. Heat oil in a medium saucepan over medium heat. Stir in flour; cook, stirring constantly, 1½ minutes. Stir in tomatillo purée. Cook, uncovered, 3 more minutes. Cover and keep warm over low heat.

4. Place 2 tortillas between damp paper towels. Microwave tortillas at HIGH 15 seconds. Repeat procedure with remaining tortillas. Spoon ½ cup chicken down center of each tortilla; roll up tortillas, and place, seam sides down, in a lightly greased 11- x 7-inch baking dish. Pour tomatillo sauce over enchiladas.

5. Cover and bake at 400° for 10 minutes. Remove from oven, and sprinkle with queso fresco. Let stand 5 minutes before serving. Garnish, if desired. **Makes 4 servings.**

Chiles Poblanos

Though Texas poblanos can grow pretty large, medium-size chiles are ideal for this recipe.

16   wooden picks
3   Tbsp. olive oil, divided
½   cup chopped onion
½   tsp. minced garlic
2   cups shredded cooked chicken
2   cups (8 oz.) shredded mozzarella cheese
½   tsp. black pepper
8   poblano chile peppers

1. Soak wooden picks in water 30 minutes; drain. Heat 1 Tbsp. oil in a skillet over medium-high heat. Sauté onion and garlic in hot oil 5 minutes or until tender. Remove from heat; cool. Stir in chicken, cheese, and black pepper.

2. Preheat grill to 400° to 450° (high) heat. Cut tops off poblanos, and remove seeds and stems using a paring knife or kitchen shears. Stuff chicken-cheese filling evenly into poblanos. Secure tops of peppers with wooden picks. Brush stuffed peppers with remaining 2 Tbsp. oil.

3. Grill, covered with grill lid, 15 to 17 minutes or until charred and tender. (Do not turn peppers.)

Makes 4 servings.

Candylicious

Houston, Texas

This teeny tiny candy store is big on sweet nostalgia. Candy cigarettes (remember when those were actually cool?), wax lips, and classic Clark Bars you probably figured had expired long ago are mixed in with more novel offerings like hamburger-shaped gummies, chocolate Skittles, and massive candy topiaries that are perfect for a party or a post-breakup, self-induced sugar coma. Get your fix at 1837 West Alabama Street.

Food Find:

Henry's Puffy Tacos

San Antonio, Texas

Lat./Long. 29.48349,-98.604605

6030 Bandera Road 78238

(210) 432-7341

www.henryspuffytacos.com

Don't Miss:

The Smoky Salsa

Bowls of the stuff arrive at your table, and next thing you know you've snarfed down a pound of chips and salsa. It's that good!

San Antonio is home to the Alamo, the river walk, and the puffy taco, and Henry's makes the best in town. The "puff" in this case happens when a raw corn masa tortilla is deep fried in a vat of oil until it creates a delicate, crackly shell that is shaped to cradle the taco filling of your choosing. Add a few spoonfuls of hot red salsa and a frozen margarita and you're in Tex-Mex heaven. An ice cold cerveza is an equally worthy companion.

Salsa Quemada

Reduce the burn in this smoky salsa by seeding the jalapeños after grilling.

6   large tomatoes
10   large jalapeño peppers
1   large white onion, peeled and halved
2   large garlic cloves, unpeeled
1   tsp. salt
Tortilla chips

1. Coat cold cooking grate of grill with cooking spray, and place on grill. Place first 4 ingredients on cooking grate. Grill, covered with grill lid, 15 to 20 minutes or until slightly charred, turning once. Remove vegetables from grill; let cool slightly. Peel garlic; remove stems and, if desired, seeds from peppers.

2. Pulse vegetables, in 2 batches, in a food processor 5 times or just until chopped. Pour salsa to a large bowl; stir in salt. Serve with tortilla chips. **Makes 6 cups.**

✻ Diner Secret: A good char gives this hot salsa the addictive flavors of smoke and fire.

* Diner Secret: Browning rice in oil helps keep the grains fluffy and separate.

Chicken Tortilla Soup with Rice

4   skinned, bone-in chicken breasts
1   Tbsp. vegetable oil
2   cups uncooked extra long–grain rice
1   cup chopped onion
1   cup chopped green bell pepper
2   tsp. salt, divided
2½ tsp. ground cumin, divided
½   tsp. garlic powder
⅛   tsp. pepper
3   (8-oz.) cans tomato sauce, divided
2   tsp. garlic salt
¾   tsp. pepper
Garnishes: diced tomato, diced avocado, shredded
        Monterey Jack cheese, tortilla chips

1. Combine 7 cups water and chicken in a Dutch oven. Bring to a boil; cover, reduce heat, and simmer 15 minutes or until chicken is tender. Remove chicken from broth, reserving broth; strain and set aside until cool enough to touch.
2. Meanwhile, heat oil in a large saucepan over medium-high heat. Add rice, onion, and bell pepper; sauté 4 minutes. Stir in 1 tsp. salt, ½ tsp. cumin, garlic powder, and ⅛ tsp. pepper. Stir in 3¼ cups water and 1 can tomato sauce. Cover and bring to a boil; reduce heat, and simmer 20 minutes or until liquid is absorbed and rice is tender.
3. Skin and bone chicken. Shred chicken; return chicken to broth. Stir in remaining 1 tsp. salt, remaining 2 tsp. cumin, remaining 2 cans tomato sauce, garlic salt, and ¾ tsp. pepper. Bring soup to a boil; remove from heat. Spoon rice into soup bowls, and ladle soup over rice. Garnish, if desired. **Makes 6 to 8 cups.**

Greetings from VIRGINIA

State Capitol in Richmond

State Flower

7222

Lush rhododendron and evergreens grace the peaks and valleys of the Blue Ridge Mountains.

Virginia

Best Drive

Blue Ridge Parkway

What's a collection of drives without America's favorite, the Blue Ridge Parkway? Ambling more than 400 miles along the Appalachian Mountains, the Parkway is legendary for its easy roads, slow speeds, gorgeous vistas, comfortable stops, plus its stunning collection of trees, bushes, wildflowers, and animals. You could travel an entire continent and not see as many bird varieties. My favorite section is the Skyline Drive, which winds from Waynesboro to Front Royal. Make sure to check the weather before venturing up that high. **Length:** 469 miles (105 from Waynesboro to Front Royal)

Mom's Apple Pie Company

Leesburg, Virginia

GPS COORDINATES:
Lat./Long. 39.112768,-77.55969

220 Loudoun Street Southeast 20176
(703) 771-8590
www.momsapplepieco.com

Don't Miss:

Macaroons

I'm a fan of macaroons. Not only are Mom's creamy on the inside and crunchy on the outside (as the good Lord intended), they're a snap to make in your own kitchen.

BLUEBERR

The fruit comes straight from the owner's farm. Preservatives and tons of sugar are a no-no at Mom's Apple Pie Company. Love goes straight into every pie and pastry. You can't mass-produce this sort of thing, so Mom's remains one of those small, tucked-away treasures you won't want to miss. Whether you've a taste for apple, pumpkin, raspberry, rhubarb, or blueberry pie, you'll find it among the company's well-worn wooden walls and rustic atmosphere.

Blueberry Pie

1	cup sugar
¼	cup minute tapioca
⅛	tsp. salt
2	lb. frozen wild blueberries (6 cups)
1	Tbsp. fresh lemon juice
Piecrust (page 235)
1	large egg
3	Tbsp. sugar

1. Combine sugar, tapioca, and salt in a large bowl; toss well. Add blueberries and lemon juice, tossing to coat.
2. Preheat oven to 375°. Roll 1 piecrust dough disk to ⅛-inch thickness (about 13 inches wide) on a lightly floured surface. Gently press dough into a 9-inch pie plate. Spoon blueberry mixture into crust, mounding in center.
3. Roll remaining dough disk to ⅛-inch thickness (about 13 inches wide). Gently place dough over filling; fold edges under, and crimp, sealing to bottom crust. Combine egg and 3 Tbsp. sugar, stirring well. Brush egg mixture over top crust. Cut 4 to 5 slits in top of pie for steam to escape.

4. Bake at 375° on an oven rack one-third up from bottom of oven 1 hour. Cover loosely with aluminum foil, and bake 15 minutes. Transfer to a wire rack, and cool 4 hours before serving. **Makes 8 servings.**

Mom's Apple Pie

Mom's pies have been touted as some of the best in the South. This apple version is no exception.

1	cup sugar
2	Tbsp. cornstarch
1	tsp. ground cinnamon
¼	tsp. salt
3	lb. York apples*, peeled, cored, and cut into ½-inch-thick wedges

Piecrust

| 1 | large egg |
| 2 | Tbsp. sugar |

1. Combine first 4 ingredients in a large bowl; stir well. Add apple slices, tossing to coat.

2. Preheat oven to 375°. Roll each portion of piecrust dough into a 13-inch circle on a well-floured surface. Fit half of dough into a lightly greased 9-inch deep-dish pie plate. Spoon apples into crust, packing tightly and mounding in center. Fit remaining dough over apples; trim excess pastry. Fold edges under, and crimp. Cut slits in top of pie for steam to escape.

3. Combine egg and sugar; stir well. Brush egg mixture over pastry.

4. Bake at 375° on lowest rack of oven for 1 hour or until crust is golden brown, juices are thickened and bubbly, and apples are tender when pierced with a long wooden pick through slits in crust. Let

One taste of Mom's creations will make her the apple of your eye.

cool on a wire rack 2 hours before serving. **Makes 8 servings.**

*Jonagold apples may be substituted.

Piecrust

2½	cups all-purpose flour
1	Tbsp. sugar
1	tsp. salt
1	cup unsalted butter, cut into pieces
8	to 9 Tbsp. ice-cold water

1. Pulse first 3 ingredients in a food processor 3 or 4 times or until combined. Add butter pieces through food chute, and pulse 12 times or until crumbly.

2. With processor running, gradually add 6 Tbsp. ice-cold water, and process just until dough forms a ball and leaves sides of bowl, adding more water if necessary. Shape dough into 2 flat disks. Wrap in plastic wrap, and chill 2 hours. **Makes enough for 1 double-crust pie.**

The Roanoker Restaurant

Roanoke, Virginia

GPS COORDINATES:

Lat./Long. 37.252307,-79.960116

2522 Colonial Avenue 24015

(540) 344-7746

www.theroanokerrestaurant.com

Don't Miss:

Biscuits

Pioneered by Cordelia "Knookie" Clarkson, the secret to these biscuits is not to over-knead the dough. If practice doesn't make perfect, you can buy biscuits by the dozen.

How does a restaurant become an institution? For the Roanoker, its secret may be one simple dish: the classic, fluffy, Southern biscuit. Light and white on the inside, salty, buttery, and brown on the outside, the Roanoker's biscuit has been a Virginia tradition since 1941. Combined with their hearty sausage gravy (35 cents in 1941, but still a deal at $3.19 today) and a mug of the Roanoker's own blend of H&C Coffee, you have the makings to start the perfect day.

Buttermilk Biscuits

3½ cups self-rising flour
1 Tbsp. baking powder
1½ tsp. sugar
½ cup shortening
1¼ cups buttermilk
2 Tbsp. butter, melted

1. Preheat oven to 400°. Combine first 3 ingredients in a large bowl; stir well. Cut shortening into flour mixture with a pastry blender or fork until crumbly. Add buttermilk, stirring just until dry ingredients are moistened.
2. Turn dough out onto a lightly floured surface, and knead lightly 3 or 4 times. Pat dough to 1-inch thickness; cut with a 3-inch round cutter, and place on a lightly greased baking sheet.
3. Bake at 400° for 25 minutes or until golden brown. Brush tops with melted butter. **Makes 8 servings.**

To ensure light and fluffy results, don't overwork the dough.

No white tablecloths at this upscale burger joint.

Bistro on Main

Lexington, Virginia

At Bistro on Main, it's the beef. That's what makes this restaurant's Bistro Burger the best in the area and possibly tops in the entire commonwealth.

Owner Jackie Lupo buys only Virginia-grown organic beef from Polyface Farm in nearby Swoope. The 6-ounce patties are formed by hand and seared over an open flame. Fresh lettuce and sliced tomatoes, harvested in peak season, add the perfect touch. You can pile on bacon, Cheddar, mushrooms, or onion, but in my mind, you don't need all that. This burger stands alone. Stop in for a bite at 8 N. Main Street.

Food Find:

Pink Cadillac Diner

Natural Bridge, Virginia

GPS COORDINATES:
Lat./Long. 37.676635,-79.501192

4743 S. Lee Highway 24578
(540) 291-2378
www.pinkcadillacdineronline.com

Don't Miss:

The Unflappable Service

Adults will like the waitstaff's easygoing attitude: "Honey, do you want some more coffee?" And the kids will love the milkshakes and chicken tenders.

Rocket tail fins, Elvis, teal-vinyl booths, and vintage movie-star posters harken back to a day when many roadside diners and motels graced the American highway. One look at the pink 1954 Cadillac parked out front lets you know you've arrived back in time to a spot where double cheeseburgers, hearty chili, and frothy strawberry shakes fill the menu. Pop a quarter in the juke box and chow down.

Manhattan Clam Chowder

This chowder is on the spicy side. Adjust pepper amounts according to your taste.

3   bacon slices
3   baking potatoes, peeled and cut into
     ½-inch cubes
3   celery ribs, coarsely chopped
2   medium onions, coarsely chopped
1½   Tbsp. fresh thyme leaves
1   Tbsp. jarred seafood base
1   tsp. celery salt
1   tsp. freshly ground black pepper
½   tsp. ground red pepper
3   bay leaves
2   (14½-oz.) cans diced tomatoes, undrained
2   (11.5-oz.) cans vegetable juice
2   (10-oz.) cans baby clams, undrained

1. Bring 4 cups water to a boil in a large stock-pot. Meanwhile, cook bacon slices in a large skillet over medium heat 8 minutes or until crisp; remove bacon, and drain on paper towels, reserving 2 Tbsp. drippings in skillet. Crumble bacon.
2. Sauté potatoes, celery, and onion in hot drippings until celery and onion are tender. Stir in fresh thyme and next 5 ingredients; cook 1 minute. Add mixture to stockpot. Stir in tomatoes, vegetable juice, and crumbled bacon; bring to a boil. Reduce heat, and cook, uncovered, 30 minutes or until potatoes are tender. Stir in clams with liquid; cook 5 minutes or just until thoroughly heated. Remove and discard bay leaves. **Makes 13⅓ cups.**
Note: We tested with Penzey's Seafood Base.

Pink Cadillac Chili

Top this hearty chili with shredded Cheddar, sour cream, and green onions.

5   lb. ground chuck
¼   cup chili powder
2   tsp. dried crushed red pepper
1½   tsp. salt
1½   tsp. ground cumin
1½   tsp. dried oregano
1½   tsp. freshly ground pepper
2   garlic cloves, minced
1   green bell pepper, chopped
1   medium onion, chopped
4   (16-oz.) cans dark red kidney beans, drained
     and rinsed
2   (29-oz.) cans tomato sauce
1   Tbsp. jarred beef soup base
1   Tbsp. browning-and-seasoning sauce

1. Brown ground beef in a 12-qt. stockpot or Dutch oven over high heat, stirring often, 10 to 15 minutes or until meat crumbles and is no longer pink; drain. Return meat to pot. Add chili powder and next 8 ingredients; cook over medium-high heat 6 to 8 minutes or until vegetables are tender.
2. Add beans and remaining ingredients. Bring to a boil; reduce heat, and simmer, uncovered, 10 minutes, stirring occasionally. **Makes 20 cups.**

The Local

Charlottesville, Virginia

GPS COORDINATES:
Lat./Long. 38.024455,-78.475554

824 Hinton Avenue 22902

(434) 984-9749

www.thelocal-cville.com

Don't Miss:

"Not Hot Chocolate"

The "Not Hot Chocolate" is a little bit of sin in a coffee cup. Dense cream, rich chocolate, and just the right chill make this dessert an absolutely decadent way to finish any meal.

Warm wooden walls, incredibly fresh ingredients, and two outdoor porches make The Local one of my favorite spots in Virginia. Charlottesville has an amazing dining scene to begin with, but this restaurant takes it up a notch. The inventive menu pushes in-season offerings. I adore The Local's trout (be warned—it comes with the head and tail, if that sort of thing freaks you out), which is stuffed with Spanish sausage and Parmesan and served over a fresh corn salad. If it's on the menu when you visit, make sure to give it a try.

Red Wine-Braised Short Ribs

4½ lb. beef short ribs
Salt and pepper
¼ cup all-purpose flour
2 to 3 Tbsp. canola oil
4 medium carrots, coarsely chopped
2 celery ribs, coarsely chopped
1 yellow onion, coarsely chopped
1 large garlic bulb, peeled and separated into cloves
1 (750-ml.) bottle dry red wine
1 cup chicken broth
1 cup beef broth
½ cup lightly packed fresh thyme sprigs
3 bay leaves
⅛ tsp. black peppercorns
1½ cups white pearl onions
1½ cups red pearl onions
2 cups baby carrots with tops
1 Tbsp. canola oil
½ cup butter, divided
2 lb. Yukon gold potatoes
⅓ cup whipping cream
1 tsp. salt
Garnishes: fresh thyme leaves, chopped fresh parsley

1. Preheat oven to 350°. Sprinkle ribs with desired amount of salt and pepper. Dredge in flour, shaking off excess. Brown ribs, in batches, in hot oil in a Dutch oven over medium-high heat 5 minutes on each side. Drain and transfer browned ribs to a 13- x 9-inch baking dish. Cover and set aside.
2. Add chopped carrots, celery, yellow onion, and garlic to Dutch oven; sauté over medium-high heat 3 to 4 minutes. Add wine, stirring to loosen particles from bottom of pan. Simmer, uncovered, 15 minutes, stirring occasionally, or until wine is reduced by half. Add chicken and beef broth; bring to a boil. Remove from heat. Gradually pour wine and vegetable mixture over ribs in dish. Sprinkle with ½ cup thyme sprigs, bay leaves, and peppercorns. Cover tightly with aluminum foil.
3. Bake at 350° for 2½ to 3 hours or until meat is very tender.
4. Meanwhile, cook pearl onions in boiling salted water to cover 2 to 3 minutes or just until crisp-tender; drain, cool slightly, and peel.
5. Remove ribs from baking dish to a serving platter. Cover and keep warm. Increase oven temperature to 400°. Arrange baby carrots on a jelly-roll pan; drizzle with 1 Tbsp. oil. Bake at 400° for 40 minutes or until tender, stirring once after 30 minutes.
6. Meanwhile, strain sauce from baking dish into a saucepan, discarding vegetables and thyme. Cook sauce over high heat, stirring often, 10 minutes or until reduced by half and slightly thickened. Add ¼ cup butter, 1 Tbsp. at a time, whisking until blended after each addition. Remove from heat.
7. Bring potatoes and cold water to cover to a boil in a large Dutch oven over medium-high heat; boil 20 to 25 minutes or until tender. Drain; peel, if desired. Mash together potatoes, cream, remaining ¼ cup butter, and 1 tsp. salt.
8. Arrange roasted carrots around ribs on platter. Spoon desired amount of sauce over ribs and carrots. Garnish platter, if desired. Serve remaining sauce over ribs and mashed potatoes. **Makes 6 servings.**

Ham and Vegetable Hash with Hollandaise

The hash is the star in this dish, containing two of The Local's favorite ingredients, Blue Crab and Country Ham.

Hash

1	lb. sweet potatoes
1	lb. Yukon gold potatoes
1	Tbsp. olive oil
1	tsp. salt
½	tsp. freshly ground pepper
½	yellow onion, thinly sliced
2	Tbsp. butter
4	oz. country ham, thinly sliced
½	lb. fresh lump crabmeat, drained
2	green onions, sliced

Old Bay Hollandaise

3	pasteurized eggs
2½	Tbsp. lemon juice
½	cup butter, melted
½	tsp. Old Bay seasoning
¼	tsp. salt

Seared Rockfish

2	lb. Rockfish or grouper fillets (6 fillets)
½	tsp. salt
½	tsp. freshly ground pepper
1	Tbsp. olive oil

Arugula Salad

2	Tbsp. lemon juice
2	Tbsp. extra virgin olive oil
⅛	tsp. salt
⅛	tsp. pepper
1	(5-oz.) package arugula

It only looks fancy. Humble...and local... ingredients come together with panache at The Local.

Produce from Virginia's fertile farmland makes a daily appearance on the menu.

1. **Prepare Hash:** Preheat oven to 450°. Peel both types potatoes; dice. Toss with 1 Tbsp. oil; season with salt and pepper. Arrange in a single layer on a large rimmed baking sheet. Bake at 450° for 20 minutes or until just tender.

2. Sauté yellow onion in 2 Tbsp. butter over medium-high heat 2 minutes. Add ham; sauté 2 minutes. Add roasted potatoes; cook 2 minutes. Stir in crabmeat and green onion. Cook 1 minute or just until crabmeat is thoroughly heated. Remove from heat; keep warm.

3. **Prepare Old Bay Hollandaise:** Separate eggs, reserving whites for another use. Place egg yolks

and lemon juice in a blender. Turn blender on medium; gradually add melted butter in a slow, steady stream. Add Old Bay seasoning and ¼ tsp. salt. Set aside.

4. Prepare Seared Rockfish: Sprinkle fish with ½ tsp. each salt and pepper. Heat 1 Tbsp. oil in a large nonstick skillet over medium-high heat. Add fish pieces; cook 2 to 3 minutes on each side or until golden. Reduce heat to medium; cook 2 to 3 more minutes or until fish flakes with a fork.

5. Prepare Arugula Salad: Whisk together 2 Tbsp. lemon juice and next 3 ingredients. Drizzle olive oil mixture over arugula; toss to coat.

6. Divide sweet potato hash between 6 dinner plates, top each with fish. Spoon hollandaise onto each plate. Top fish evenly with arugula. Serve immediately. **Makes 6 servings.**

Note: We tested with pasteurized egg yolks for this Old Bay Hollandaise since the sauce is not cooked. The pasteurized yolks make the sauce safe for consumption. Find pasteurized eggs in shells in a carton in the refrigerated section with other eggs.

Rubbernecker Wonder:
Chancellorsville, Virginia

Chancellorsville Battlefield

General Thomas Jonathan "Stonewall" Jackson is considered one of the most brilliant military strategists in American history. Tragically, he was shot in the left arm by "friendly fire" (which is anything but friendly) after the Battle of Chancellorsville, and the arm was amputated. Upon hearing the news, General Lee sent a message "Give General Jackson my affectionate regards, and say to him: he has lost his left arm but I my right." That arm was buried in a nearby field, and the marker may be visited at the Chancellorsville Battlefield visitor's center.

Virginia is the land of gentlemen farmers and equestrians.

Look!

GREETINGS from WEST VIRGINIA

State Capitol in Charleston

State Flower
the Rhododendron

West Virginia

Best Drive

Cheat River Byway

Though it's just under 15 miles long, this part of West Virginia Route 72 sports gorgeous views and vistas of the state's natural beauty. Not only is much of the area here in northern West Virginia unpopulated, it also is unspoiled by strip malls and gasaterias. On parts of the road, you may think you're the last car on earth—it's that uncrowded. The Cheat River Canyon is also mostly free and wild, so you'll see excellent glimpses of the region at its best.

Length: 14.3 miles

Stardust Cafe

Lewisburg, West Virginia

GPS COORDINATES:
Lat./Long. 37.8017,-80.445383

102 East Washington Street 24901
(304) 647-3663
www.stardustcafewv.com

Don't Miss:

This Place

Stardust Cafe took the space formerly occupied by Clingman's Market. The owner decided to keep the window lettering for good luck and sentimental reasons. Be sure to try the coffee here. Stardust opened originally as a coffee shop and their brews are the best in town.

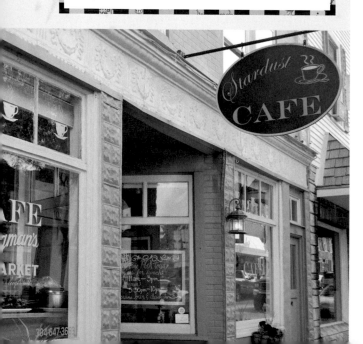

When a restaurateur talks passionately about her farmers and supplies, and she knows the farmers by name, you can bet you're in for a delicious meal. Owner Sparrow Huffman's exuberance touches on every aspect of the Stardust Cafe. The clean modern décor has a cozy feel and a sentimental history. Dishes range from light and organic to hearty and robust. As a result, everyone from ladies-who-lunch to off-duty contractors feel right at home here.

The Trust Me Salad

Cranberry granola is a welcome surprise in this colorful salad.

1   (22-oz.) package romaine lettuce hearts
1   cup cranberry granola
2   large ripe tomatoes, cut into thin wedges
2   avocados, chopped
1   medium-size red onion, thinly sliced
1   (4-oz.) package goat cheese, crumbled
½   cup balsamic vinegar
3   Tbsp. coarse-grained mustard
2   Tbsp. honey
½   tsp. salt
¼   tsp. pepper
2   garlic cloves, minced
1   cup extra virgin olive oil

1. Wash romaine hearts; tear into bite-size pieces. Combine romaine and next 5 ingredients in a large serving bowl; toss gently.

2. Combine vinegar and next 5 ingredients in a 2-cup glass measuring cup; whisk until blended. Add oil in a slow, steady stream, whisking constantly until smooth. Drizzle desired amount of dressing over salad; toss to coat. **Makes 8 to 10 servings.**

✱ Diner Secret: The usual mayo slather gets gourmet with a bit of pesto blended in.

The Aaron

This grilled chicken sandwich piles on the pesto and crispy bacon.

1   (6-oz.) skinned and boned chicken breast
¼   tsp. salt
¼   tsp. pepper
2   honey-whole wheat bread slices, toasted
Pesto
Mayonnaise
3   cooked bacon slices
2   green leaf lettuce leaves
2   tomato slices
Thinly sliced red onion

1. Preheat grill to 350° to 400° (medium-high) heat. Sprinkle both sides of chicken breast with salt and pepper. Grill chicken, covered with grill lid, 4 to 6 minutes on each side or until done. Remove from grill; slice chicken, if desired.
2. Spread desired amount of pesto and mayonnaise on 1 side of each bread slice. Layer 1 bread slice, mayonnaise side up, with grilled chicken, bacon, lettuce, tomato, and onion. Top with remaining bread slice, mayonnaise side down.
Makes 1 serving.

Stewart's Drive-In
Huntington, West Virginia

Wheel your car into this Huntington classic, roll down your window, and prepare to devour a pile of hot dogs as big as your head. Stewart's has delivered them the same way since 1932: hot, delicious, and rolled in a napkin (which is an ingenious way to keep their moist, steamy goodness). A side of chili-cheese fries, which are soggy in a good way, must be washed down with a root beer or frosty shake.

Stewart's slogan remains, "If you're going to be original, you can count on being copied!" Stewart's has copied itself, actually, but the original location is still going. Its simple wooden structure, Depression-era light fixtures, and charming touches like Coca-Cola in an original glass bottle somehow make the dogs taste better. Stop by and get yourself a dog at the one that started it all: 2445 5th Avenue.

Food Find:

West Virginia

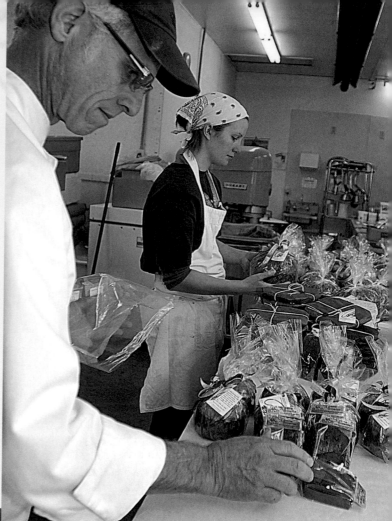

The Crazy Baker

Renick, West Virginia

GPS COORDINATES:

Lat./Long. 38.013254,-80.376323

218 Crane Road 24966

(866) 440-4797

www.thecrazybaker.com

Don't Miss:

The Panforte

This thin, Italian cake made from almonds is awesome for a road trip. It's a much healthier alternative to gas station beef sticks and processed cheese when you get the munchies.

The Crazy Baker is bonkers over quality ingredients. When Hall Hitzig starts his famous granola, he begins with the finest oats, fruits, honey, and nuts. And when you bite into his sticky toffee pudding, you'll start talking all out of your head, too, because it's made with what tastes like a metric ton of high-quality butter, sugar, and flour. It's a bite of JOE (Jolly Olde England) right on your fork—or better yet, spoon.

You may visit the Crazy Baker, but there's no sit-down restaurant. The best idea? Order by phone: (866) 440-4797.

Pecan Panna Cotta

Pecans lend pale color and a deep but subtle flavor to this soft molded dessert.

3   cups milk, divided
2¼ cups finely chopped pecans
1   cup whipping cream
1   vanilla bean, split lengthwise
2   envelopes unflavored gelatin
½   cup sugar
Garnish: pecan halves

1. Bring 2 cups milk and next 3 ingredients just to a simmer in a medium saucepan. Reduce heat to low; cook over low heat 25 minutes, stirring occasionally. Strain; discard pecans. Return strained milk mixture to saucepan. Scrape seeds from vanilla bean into cream mixture with back of a knife.
2. Meanwhile, sprinkle gelatin over 1 cup milk, and let stand 10 minutes. Add to strained mixture in saucepan, and cook over medium-low heat, stirring constantly, 5 minutes or until gelatin dissolves. Increase heat to medium; add sugar, and stir until sugar dissolves (about 2 to 3 minutes). Remove from heat.
3. Divide mixture among 7 (6-oz.) custard cups. Cover and chill 2½ hours to 2 days. Gently run a small knife around outer edge of each custard cup to break seal. Dip bottom of each cup in warm water for about 15 seconds. Unmold desserts onto serving plates, and carefully remove cups. Garnish, if desired. Makes 7 servings.

Rubbernecker Wonder:
Thomas, West Virginia
The Purple Fiddle

If Appalachian melodies have you doing a double take as you drive through Thomas, put the car in park and join the patrons at The Purple Fiddle which hosts a toe-tapping good time on Friday, Saturday, and Sunday nights. Performers with acoustic instruments—banjo, mandolin, and, of course, fiddle—strum out folk, gospel, and original songs. From the stage, musicians peer out on a mix of fans—blue hair and Mohawks, tykes in SpongeBob pajamas, teens in AC/DC shirts, and D.C. politicos with ties slung loosely around their necks. Owner John Bright is grateful for the mix of customers. "We call this a living room atmosphere," he says. "We wanted a place you can take your 5-year-old son, watch him dance, and feel comfortable—feel safe." Drop on in and have a listen to the local music scene at 21 East Avenue.

Look!

Wheat-Free Blueberry Financiers

Each buttery-crisp almond cake has moist insides hugging a blueberry.

½   cup butter
1   cup almond flour
½   cup granulated sugar
2   Tbsp. cornstarch
2   large eggs, lightly beaten
1½   tsp. dark rum
½   tsp. vanilla extract
½   tsp. lemon zest
24   blueberries
1   cup powdered sugar
1   Tbsp. dark rum

1. Preheat oven to 350°. Melt butter in a heavy saucepan over medium heat. Cook 5 to 10 minutes or just until butter begins to brown and develop a nutty aroma. Remove from heat; skim off foam. Pour through a fine wire-mesh strainer into a small bowl; cool completely.

2. Spread almond flour in a thin layer on a baking sheet. Bake at 350° for 8 minutes or until lightly browned. Cool completely.

3. Increase oven temperature to 400°. Lightly butter 2 (12-cup) miniature muffin pans.

4. Combine almond flour, granulated sugar, and cornstarch in a bowl. Add browned butter, eggs, and next 3 ingredients, stirring until blended.

5. Spoon batter into prepared pans, filling ⅔ full. Place 1 blueberry in center of each cup. Bake at 400° for 11 minutes or until cakes spring back when touched. Cool in pans 5 minutes on wire racks; remove from pans and cool completely on wire racks.

6. While cakes cool, combine powdered sugar, 1 Tbsp. rum and 1 Tbsp. water; stirring until smooth. Drizzle glaze over cakes. **Makes 21 cakes.**

Food Festivals

Alabama

National Peanut Festival
www.nationalpeanutfestival.com
Every November in Dothan, AL

Birmingham Greek Food Festival
www.birminghamgreekfestival.net
Every September in Birmingham, AL

Arkansas

Alma Spinach Festival
www.almaspinachfestival.com
Every April in Alma, AR

Bradley County Pink Tomato Festival
www.bradleypinktomato.com
Every June in Warren, AR

Florida

Florida Strawberry Festival
www.flstrawberryfestival.com
Every March in Plant City, FL

Florida Seafood Festival
www.floridaseafoodfestival.com
Every November in Apalachicola, FL

Georgia

Vidalia Onion Festival
www.vidaliaonionfestival.com
Every April in Vidalia, GA

Wild Georgia Shrimp Festival
(912) 635-3636
Every September in Jekyll Island, GA

Kentucky

Spoonbread Festival
www.spoonbreadfestival.com
Every September in Berea, KY

The Kentucky Bourbon Festival
www.kybourbonfestival.com
Every September in Bardstown, KY

Louisiana

Washington Catfish Festival
(337) 826-3626
Every May in Washington, LA

Louisiana Crawfish Festival
www.louisianacrawfishfestival.com
Every March in Chalmette, LA

Maryland

Maryland Seafood Festival
www.mdseafoodfestival.com
Every September in Sandy Point, MD

Autumn Wine Festival
www.autumnwinefestival.org
Every October in Salisbury, MD

Mississippi

Slugburger Festival
www.slugburgerfestival.com
Every July in Corinth, MS

Annual Mississippi Watermelon Festival
www.mswatermelonfestival.com
Every July in Mize, MS

Missouri

Rock'n Ribs BBQ Festival
www.rocknribs.com
Every April in Springfield, MO

Annual Great Stone Hill Grape Stomp
www.stonehillwinery.com
Every August in Hermann, MO

North Carolina

North Carolina Pickle Festival
www.ncpicklefest.org
Every April in Mount Olive, NC

North Carolina Potato Festival
www.ncpotatofestival.com
Every May in Elizabeth City, NC

Oklahoma

Porter Peach Festival
www.porterpeachfestival.com
Every July in Porter, OK

Pumpkin Festival
(580) 832-3538
Every October in Cordell, OK

South Carolina

World Grits Festival
www.worldgritsfestival.com
Every April in St. George, SC

Rosewood Crawfish Festival
www.rosewoodcrawfishfestival.com
Every May in Columbia, SC

South Carolina Poultry Festival
www.scpoultryfestival.com
Every May in Batesburg-Leesville, SC

Virginia

Chocolate Lovers Festival
www.chocolatefestival.net
Every March in Fairfax, VA

Pork, Peanut, & Pine Festival
www.porkpeanutpinefestival.org
Every July in Surry, VA

West Virginia

Blackberry Festival
www.wvblackberry.com
Every August in Nutter Fort, WV

Taste of Appalachian
www.appalachianfestival.net
Every August in Beckley, WV

Metric Equivalents

The recipes that appear in this cookbook use the standard U.S. method for measuring liquid and dry or solid ingredients (teaspoons, tablespoons, and cups). The information in the following charts is provided to help cooks outside the United States successfully use these recipes. All equivalents are approximate.

Metric Equivalents for Different Types of Ingredients

A standard cup measure of a dry or solid ingredient will vary in weight depending on the type of ingredient. A standard cup of liquid is the same volume for any type of liquid. Use the following chart when converting standard cup measures to grams (weight) or milliliters (volume).

Standard Cup	Fine Powder (ex. flour)	Grain (ex. rice)	Granular (ex. sugar)	Liquid Solids (ex. butter)	Liquid (ex. milk)
1	140 g	150 g	190 g	200 g	240 ml
¾	105 g	113 g	143 g	150 g	180 ml
⅔	93 g	100 g	125 g	133 g	160 ml
½	70 g	75 g	95 g	100 g	120 ml
⅓	47 g	50 g	63 g	67 g	80 ml
¼	35 g	38 g	48 g	50 g	60 ml
⅛	18 g	19 g	24 g	25 g	30 ml

Useful Equivalents for Dry Ingredients by Weight

(To convert ounces to grams, multiply the number of ounces by 30.)

1 oz	=	¹⁄₁₆ lb	=	30 g
4 oz	=	¼ lb	=	120 g
8 oz	=	½ lb	=	240 g
12 oz	=	¾ lb	=	360 g
16 oz	=	1 lb	=	480 g

Useful Equivalents for Length

(To convert inches to centimeters, multiply the number of inches by 2.5.)

1 in			=	2.5 cm		
6 in	=	½ ft	=	15 cm		
12 in	=	1 ft	=	30 cm		
36 in	=	3 ft	= 1 yd =	90 cm		
40 in			=	100 cm	=	1 m

Useful Equivalents for Liquid Ingredients by Volume

¼ tsp					=	1 ml	
½ tsp					=	2 ml	
1 tsp					=	5 ml	
3 tsp	=	1 Tbsp		=	½ fl oz =	15 ml	
		2 Tbsp	= ⅛ cup	=	1 fl oz =	30 ml	
		4 Tbsp	= ¼ cup	=	2 fl oz =	60 ml	
		5⅓ Tbsp	= ⅓ cup	=	3 fl oz =	80 ml	
		8 Tbsp	= ½ cup	=	4 fl oz =	120 ml	
		10⅔ Tbsp	= ⅔ cup	=	5 fl oz =	160 ml	
		12 Tbsp	= ¾ cup	=	6 fl oz =	180 ml	
		16 Tbsp	= 1 cup	=	8 fl oz =	240 ml	
		1 pt	= 2 cups	=	16 fl oz =	480 ml	
		1 qt	= 4 cups	=	32 fl oz =	960 ml	
					33 fl oz =	1000 ml	= 1 l

Useful Equivalents for Cooking/Oven Temperatures

	Fahrenheit	Celsius	Gas Mark
Freeze water	32° F	0° C	
Room temperature	68° F	20° C	
Boil water	212° F	100° C	
Bake	325° F	160° C	3
	350° F	180° C	4
	375° F	190° C	5
	400° F	200° C	6
	425° F	220° C	7
	450° F	230° C	8
Broil			Grill

Index

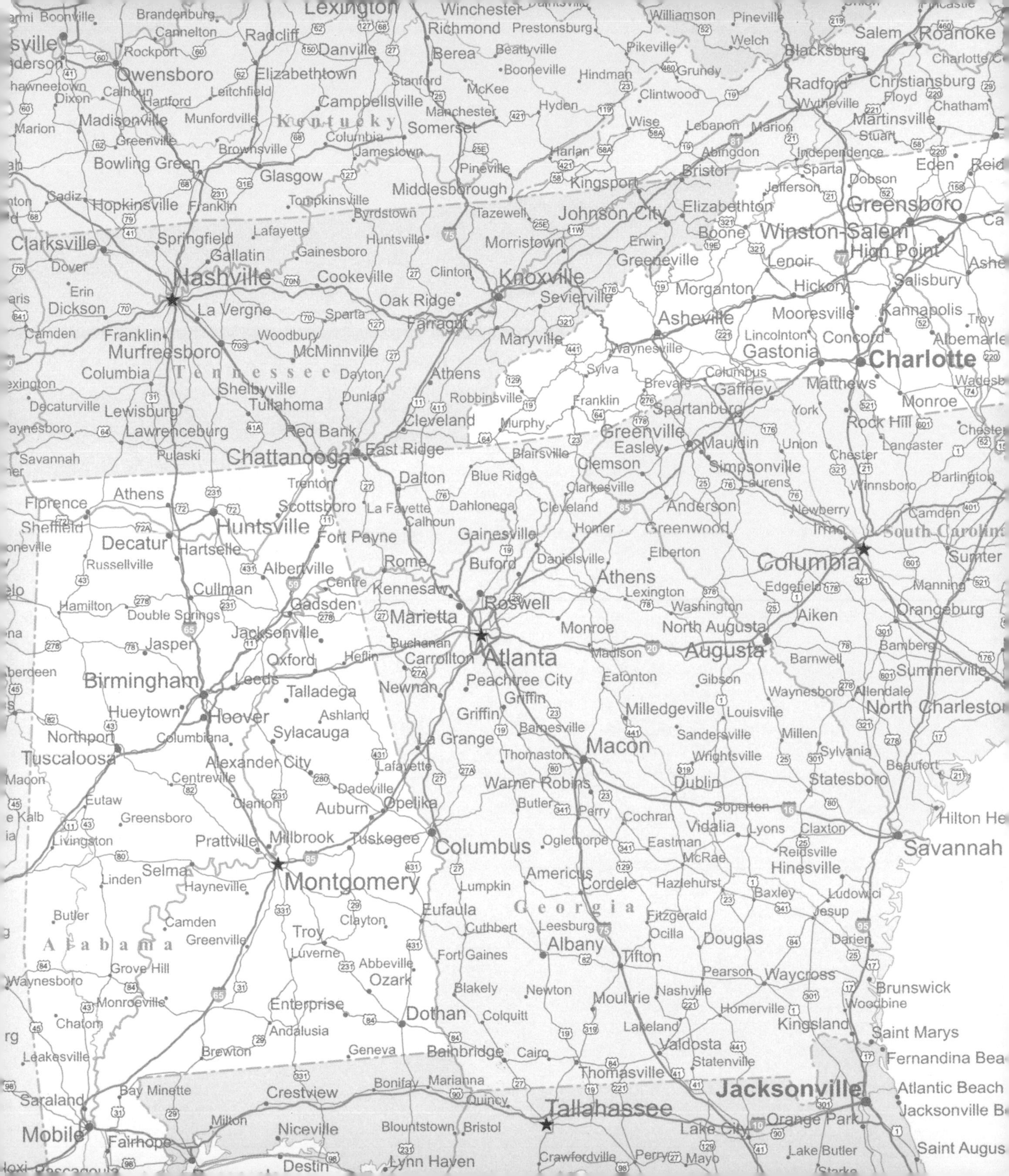

Lexington
Winchester
Richmond
Prestonsburg
Williamson
Pineville
Brandenburg
Cannelton
Radcliff
Danville
Berea
Beattyville
Pikeville
Welch
Salem
Roanoke
Rockport
Owensboro
Elizabethtown
Booneville
Hindman
Grundy
Blacksburg
Stanford
McKee
Radford
Christiansburg
Calhoun
Leitchfield
Hartford
Campbellsville
Clintwood
Wytheville
Floyd
Chatham
Madisonville
Munfordville
Kentucky
Manchester
Hyden
Martinsville
Somerset
Wise
Lebanon
Marion
Stuart
Greenville
Columbia
Brownsville
Jamestown
Harlan
Abingdon
Independence
Bowling Green
Glasgow
Pineville
Bristol
Sparta
Eden
Reid
Jefferson
Dobson
Hopkinsville
Franklin
Middlesborough
Kingsport
Tompkinsville
Byrdstown
Tazewell
Johnson City
Elizabethton
Greensboro
Boone
Winston-Salem
High Point
Clarksville
Springfield
Lafayette
Huntsville
Morristown
Erwin
Gallatin
Gainesboro
Greeneville
Lenoir
Dover
Nashville
Cookeville
Clinton
Knoxville
Morganton
Hickory
Salisbury
Erin
Dickson
La Vergne
Oak Ridge
Sevierville
Sparta
Asheville
Mooresville
Kannapolis
Franklin
Murfreesboro
Woodbury
Farragut
Maryville
Lincolnton
Concord
McMinnville
Gastonia
Charlotte
Columbia
Tennessee
Dayton
Athens
Sylva
Columbus
Gaffney
Matthews
Shelbyville
Brevard
Tullahoma
Dunlap
Robbinsville
Franklin
Spartanburg
Monroe
Lewisburg
Cleveland
Murphy
York
Rock Hill
Lawrenceburg
Red Bank
Greenville
Mauldin
Union
Lancaster
Pulaski
Chattanooga
East Ridge
Blairsville
Easley
Savannah
Clemson
Simpsonville
Chester
Blue Ridge
Darlington
Dalton
Trenton
Laurens
Clarkesville
Winnsboro
Florence
Athens
Scottsboro
La Fayette
Dahlonega
Cleveland
Anderson
Newberry
Calhoun
Camden
Sheffield
Huntsville
Homer
Greenwood
Fort Payne
Gainesville
Irmo
Decatur
Hartselle
South Carolina
Russellville
Albertville
Rome
Buford
Danielsville
Elberton
Columbia
Sumter
Centre
Athens
Cullman
Kennesaw
Edgefield
Manning
Hamilton
Gadsden
Roswell
Lexington
Washington
Double Springs
Marietta
Orangeburg
Jacksonville
Monroe
North Augusta
Aiken
Jasper
Buchanan
Madison
Augusta
Bamberg
Oxford
Heflin
Carrollton
Atlanta
Barnwell
Aberdeen
Birmingham
Leeds
Eatonton
Gibson
Summerville
Talladega
Newnan
Peachtree City
Waynesboro
Allendale
Griffin
Milledgeville
Louisville
North Charleston
Hueytown
Ashland
Griffin
Hoover
Sylacauga
Barnesville
Sandersville
Millen
Northport
Columbiana
La Grange
Macon
Tuscaloosa
Wrightsville
Sylvania
Alexander City
Thomaston
Beaufort
Centreville
Lafayette
Dublin
Statesboro
Warner Robins
Dadeville
Eutaw
Clanton
Auburn
Opelika
Butler
Perry
Soperton
Greensboro
Cochran
Vidalia
Lyons
Claxton
Hilton Head
Livingston
Millbrook
Tuskegee
Prattville
Oglethorpe
Eastman
Columbus
McRae
Reidsville
Savannah
Selma
Linden
Hayneville
Montgomery
Americus
Hinesville
Cordele
Hazlehurst
Baxley
Lumpkin
Ludowici
Georgia
Butler
Clayton
Eufaula
Camden
Troy
Fitzgerald
Jesup
Cuthbert
Leesburg
Ocilla
Greenville
Douglas
Alabama
Darien
Albany
Tifton
Luverne
Fort Gaines
Abbeville
Grove Hill
Ozark
Pearson
Waycross
Waynesboro
Brunswick
Blakely
Newton
Monroeville
Moultrie
Nashville
Woodbine
Enterprise
Chatom
Dothan
Colquitt
Homerville
Kingsland
Andalusia
Lakeland
Saint Marys
Valdosta
Leakesville
Brewton
Geneva
Bainbridge
Cairo
Statenville
Fernandina Beach
Thomasville
Bonifay
Marianna
Jacksonville
Saraland
Bay Minette
Crestview
Atlantic Beach
Quincy
Tallahassee
Jacksonville Beach
Milton
Orange Park
Mobile
Niceville
Blountstown
Bristol
Lake City
Fairhope
Saint Augustine
Lake Butler
Crawfordville
Perry
Mayo
Lynn Haven
Destin

Marion
Emporia
Garnett
Butler
Tuscumbia
Vienna
Waterloo
Hillsboro
Pinckneyville
McLeansboro
Newton
Burlington
Warsaw
Mound City
Osceola
Camdenton
Rolla
Steelville
Potosi
Chester
Benton
El Dorado
Eureka
Iola
Fort Scott
Nevada
Hermitage
Waynesville
Farmington
Carbondale
Derby
Howard
Fredonia
Stockton
Buffalo
Lebanon
Salem
Ironton
Centerville
Fredericktown
Jonesboro
Winfield
Parsons
Pittsburg
Lamar
Greenfield
Springfield
Marshfield
Houston
Jackson
Cape Girardeau
Independence
Coffeyville
Joplin
Carthage
Hartville
Eminence
Greenville
Newkirk
Miami
Neosho
Nixa
Ozark
Ava
Van Buren
Sikeston
Charleston
Bartlesville
Galena
West Plains
Alton
Poplar Bluff
Clinton
Pawhuska
Nowata
Vinita
Cassville
Forsyth
New Madrid
Pineville
Gainesville
Doniphan
Corning
Piggott
Pawnee
Owasso
Claremore
Bentonville
Rogers
Berryville
Mountain Home
Kennett
Perry
Siloam Springs
Harrison
Ash Flat
Pocahontas
Caruthersville
Stillwater
Tulsa
Broken Arrow
Springdale
Paragould
Melbourne
Guthrie
Sapulpa
Wagoner
Fayetteville
Jasper
Marshall
Jonesboro
Blytheville
Dyersburg
Bixby
Tahlequah
Batesville
Ripley
Chandler
Okmulgee
Muskogee
Arkansas
Clinton
Newport
Osceola
Harrisburg
Brownsville
Jackson
Midwest City
Okemah
Sallisaw
Van Buren
Clarksville
Heber Springs
Millington
Moore
Eufaula
Stigler
Fort Smith
Russellville
Searcy
Augusta
West Memphis
Memphis
Shawnee
Norman
Holdenville
Booneville
Danville
Conway
Forrest City
Collierville
Purcell
McAlester
Poteau
Perryville
Cabot
Des Arc
Horn Lake
Waldron
North Little Rock
Jacksonville
Marianna
Ada
Tunica
Ripley
Senatobia
Sulphur
Coalgate
Mena
Mount Ida
Benton
Little Rock
Helena
Sardis
Oxford
Atoka
Hot Springs
Stuttgart
Malvern
Pine Bluff
Mississippi R.
Batesville
Tishomingo
Antlers
Arkadelphia
Clarksdale
Water Valley
Madill
De Queen
Marietta
Hugo
Nashville
Rison
Star City
Sumner
Coffeeville
Durant
Idabel
Prescott
Fordyce
Rosedale
Cleveland
Grenada
Denison
Paris
Ashdown
Camden
Warren
Monticello
Arkansas City
Walthall
Sherman
Clarksville
Texarkana
Hampton
Greenville
Lake Village
Greenwood
Starkville
Cooper
Indianola
Vaiden
Lewisville
Magnolia
El Dorado
Hamburg
Belzoni
Lexington
Kosciusko
Greenville
Mount Vernon
Plano
Mount Pleasant
Pittsburg
Rockwall
Linden
Oak Grove
Yazoo City
Mississippi
Irving
Emory
Bastrop
Homer
Carthage
Garland
Jefferson
Lake Providence
Canton
Dallas
Quitman
Gilmer
Benton
Minden
Shreveport
Canton
Ruston
Monroe
Madison
Bossier City
Waxahachie
Longview
Vicksburg
Clinton
Brandon
Kilgore
Tyler
Jonesboro
Winnsboro
Raymond
Jackson
Ennis
Henderson
Athens
Carthage
Columbia
Corsicana
Jacksonville
Coushatta
Port Gibson
Mendenhall
Hazlehurst
Mansfield
Winnfield
Saint Joseph
Rusk
Fairfield
Center
Natchitoches
Harrisonburg
Fayette
Palestine
Jena
Brookhaven
Collins
Many
Natchez
Groesbeck
Nacogdoches
Colfax
Meadville
Hewitt
San Augustine
Pineville
Crockett
McComb
Columbia
Centerville
Marlin
Lufkin
Hemphill
Liberty
Tylertown
Leesville
Marksville
Temple
Franklin
Groveton
Woodville
Louisiana
Madisonville
Jasper
Clinton
Bogalusa
Cameron
De Ridder
Poplarville
Huntsville
Amite
Bryan
Woodville
Newton
Ville Platte
Zachary
Livingston
Hammond
Picayune
College Station
Eunice
Baton Rouge